741.6 · TWE

university college
for the creative arts

at canterbury, epsom, farnham
maidstone and rochester

Maidstone, Oakwood Park, Maidstone, Kent, ME16 8AG 01622 620120

This book is to be returned on or before the last date stamped below.
Fines will be charged on overdue books.

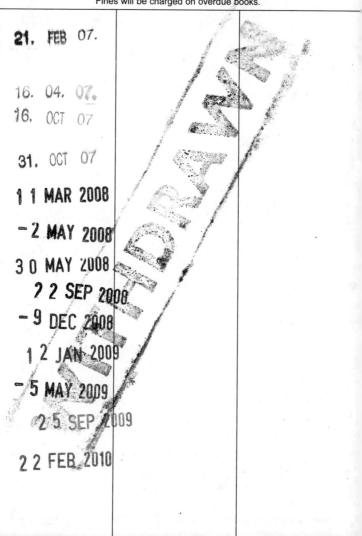

Graphic design is for business success. Graphic design is for therapy. Graphic design is for sale. Graphic design is for art and science. Graphic design is for artists not thinkers. Graphic design is for directing energy. Graphic design is for the rich. Graphic design is for kids who can't draw. Graphic design is for solving complex problems. Graphic design is for the dedicated. Graphic design is for the homepage only. Graphic design is for navigating the details. Graphic design is for a lifetime. Graphic design is for the landfill. Graphic design is for allowing the audience to participate in the process of communication. Graphic design is for users. Graphic design is for reference only. Graphic design is, for me, the beauty of life itself. Graphic design is for servicing your concept. Graphic design is for identification, information, presentation, and promotion. Graphic design is for looozers. Graphic design is for the customer. Graphic design is for women only. Graphic design is for creating a chain reaction. Graphic design is for misbehaving. Graphic design is for corporate chumps. Graphic design is for the yoga practitioner. Graphic design is for your marketing collateral. Graphic design is for graphic designers. Graphic design is for presentation purposes only. Graphic design is for sissies. Graphic design is for the revolution. Graphic design is for love+$. Graphic design is for everyone's comfort. Graphic design is for making information, ideas, and feelings tangible. Graphic design is for people who love to know how things work. Graphic design is only for left-handed people. Graphic design is for happy servants. Graphic design is for me. Graphic design is for everyone. Graphic design is for the record. Graphic design is for real.

RotoVision

Right: Gambling illustration
Designed by Sweden
Graphics for *Arena* magazine.

A RotoVision Book

Published and distributed by RotoVision SA
Route Suisse 9
CH-1295 Mies
Switzerland

RotoVision SA
Sales and Editorial Office
Sheridan House, 114 Western Road
Hove BN3 1DD, UK

Tel: +44 (0)1273 72 72 68
Fax: +44 (0)1273 72 72 69
www.rotovision.com

10 9 8 7 6 5 4 3 2 1

ISBN: 2-940361-07-X

Art Director: Tony Seddon
Designer: Jane Waterhouse

Reprographics in Singapore
by ProVision Pte. Ltd.
Tel: +65 6334 7720
Fax: +65 6334 7721

Printed in China by Midas Printing International Ltd.

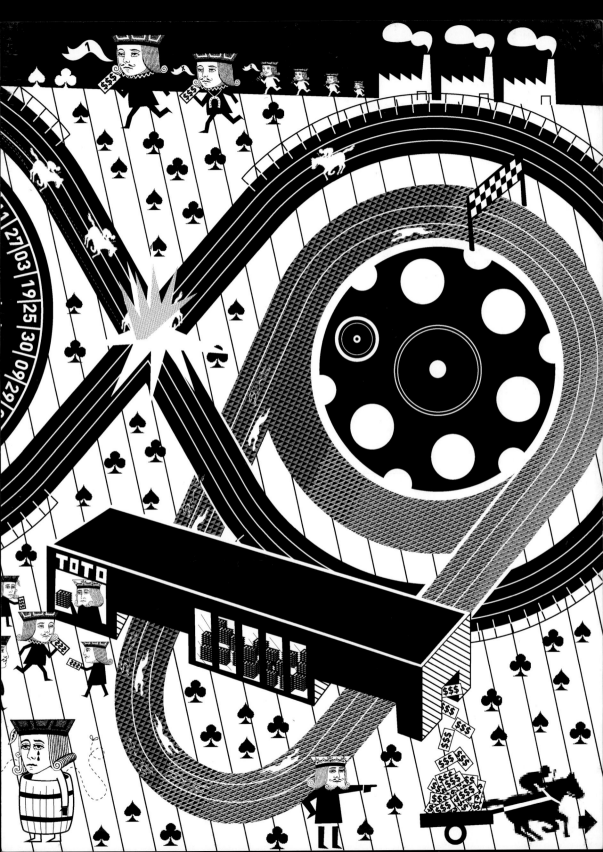

Issues

Anatomy

Portfolios

Etcetera

What is graphic design for?

You might begin by considering the question in broad terms. Graphic design is a type of language used for communicating. You use it to tell someone about something that they want, or that you think they want, or that someone else thinks they want. But things soon spiral into complexity.

It's an interesting but, ultimately, a rather odd question. You can toss in the word "anyway" and stop the conversation abruptly, or attempt to enumerate every single item and effect generated by graphic design and end up with a cataloging project on your hands like something out of a Jorge Luis Borges story.

You could begin to list things more specifically, like this: it's for selling things and ideas to make money or to further political agendas. But then you realize it's also for critiquing such behaviors. It's for making things clear—saving lives even—but it's also for enriching our everyday lives through the addition of layers of complexity, nuance, and subtlety. It's for helping people find their way and to comprehend data, but it's also for helping them to get lost in new ideas, fantastical narratives, or landscapes, and to question and contest what information is presented. Graphic design is enmeshed within all aspects of social life. From the signs that tell car drivers to stop at intersections and the nutrition label that clearly shows a consumer how much cholesterol is contained in a piece of food, to the title sequence that graphically encapsulates the atmosphere and themes of a movie to speed the viewers' suspension of belief—it is the sheer diversity and pervasiveness of graphic design's products

and outcomes—as well as their inherent contradictions—that resists their being corralled into a list for analysis.

The very idea of design having a *purpose* or being *for* something, in the context of early 21st-century society, is somewhat anachronistic. It seems to belong to an era in which ideology and fundamental truths were possible and when manifestos were proclaimed. In the first decades of the 20th-century, many designers across Europe and later in the US espoused the principles of modernism. They felt it was their duty—their moral duty—to put design's force behind the drive for social and political progress. They created systems of communication such as lowercase, sans serif alphabets that they hoped would be universally understood and would therefore improve international relations. They expressed themselves using a future-oriented graphic language that included photomontage, typo-photos, and asymmetrical composition, not because of the esthetic appeal of these elements, but because these choices flowed directly from a deeply felt sense of mission. The manifestos, writings, and work of these Modernists carved out a new and enduring role for graphic design as a medium whose very formation was linked to the political revolutions of the early decades of the 20th-century, and as a tool whose purpose was social advancement.

During WWII and the post-war period, graphic design in Europe and the US, at least, had a clear and purposeful role: to provide propaganda, camouflage, and information design on behalf of governments for the armed forces and civilians. In Britain, many

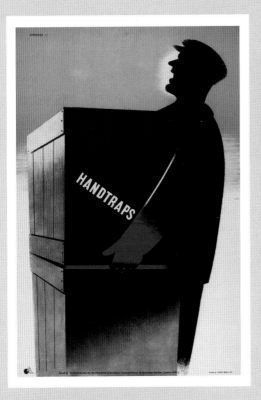

Handtraps poster
Tom Eckersley produced
numerous posters during the
1940s and 1950s promoting
worker welfare and safety.
The posters, which advocated
good maintenance of tools
and thoughtful practice in the
workplace, were commissioned
by the Royal Society for the
Prevention of Accidents and
underwritten by the newly
inaugurated Ministry of Labour.
From the collection of
Paul Rennie.

**Your Talk May Kill Your
Comrades poster**
Abram Games produced
this poster in 1942 as part
of a campaign to prevent
"Careless Talk." His message,
somewhat more hard-hitting
than earlier slogans such as
"Keep Mum, She's Not so
Dumb" or "Keep it Under
Your Hat," and delivered
with incisive visual economy,
demonstrates Games' talent
in the service of effective and
purposeful graphic design.
From the Estate of
Abram Games.

designers were involved with the nation's various efforts to reconstruct public services and to improve the quality of life. Tom Eckersley, for example—a British poster designer who drew maps for the RAF during WWII—produced numerous posters during the 1940s and 1950s promoting worker welfare and safety. F.H.K. Henrion, a German designer who emigrated to Britain in 1939, designed campaigns about health and rationing for Britain's Ministry of Information. And Abram Games, who would go on to design era-defining identities for the Festival of Britain and the BBC, developed his design skills working for the War Office, producing posters for the Auxiliary Training Service (ATS). Among the most memorable of these posters is Your Talk May Kill Your Comrades, which depicts the transformation of a soldier's words spiraling out from his open mouth into a bloody bayonet that pierces the bodies of three fellow soldiers.

In the US, Charles Coiner designed the Blue Eagle symbol for the National Recovery Administration, the federal agency created to encourage industrial recovery and combat unemployment under President Franklin D. Roosevelt, and during WWII he designed posters through the Office of War Information intended to increase worker productivity and encourage saving. This close relationship between design and the socially progressive policies of governments, public services, and even the major corporations of the day continued well after the war had ended.

In today's decentralized society, however, the responsibility for social change and progress has fallen to individuals and small groups, non-profits, and publications. Consequently the messages are more numerous and more complex. Many designers are politically motivated, of course, and are working under the radar for a host of social causes, but as design critic Rick Poynor has remarked, "Designers inevitably express the values of their day. And today's values are not primarily about social responsibility."

The issues that preoccupy contemporary practitioners include the following: maintaining a dispassionate and ironic distance from one's subject matter; the celebration of phenomena like the quotidian, ambiguity, complexity, and even absence. Also evident is a vociferous questioning of a traditionally revered model of communication in which the designer is positioned as an author, disseminator, or generator of messages and the audience a passive receiver or consumer of those messages.

Graphic design is for communicating with people: audiences, viewers, readers, users, receivers, visitors, participants, interacters, players, passers-by, experiencers, members of the public, communities, inhabitants, consumers, customers, subscribers, and clients. We encounter graphic design as groups—small ones, like local communities or special interest groups, and large ones, like populations and global consumers. The extent to which designers engage with these people—their audiences—varies dramatically. Some pay the audience no heed and design for themselves. Some design for other designers. Some design for a client's conception of the audience in question. Others find out for themselves who will be the recipients of their work, what appeals to them, and sometimes even invite their input for incorporation in the work. We'll meet designers from all these camps in the pages of this book and, through their work and thinking, examine the issues that are of critical relevance to design today and, more importantly, to the people who engage with it on a daily basis.

Right: National War Fund identity program
This symbol was designed by Charles Coiner during WWII to support the raising of funds for the war effort. From the collection of R. Roger Remington.

Left: "Production: America's Answer" poster
This poster was designed by Jean Carlu and art directed by Charles Coiner. As a volunteer consultant to the US government during WWII, Coiner contributed his services to the cause of propaganda graphics. From the collection of R. Roger Remington.

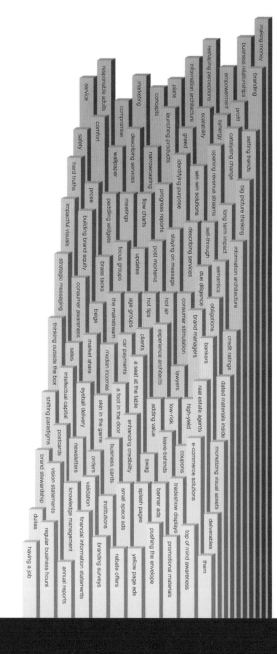

What is graphic design for?
100 answers

What is graphic design for?
100 better answers

Shawn Wolfe, Shawn Wolfe Studio, Seattle, US

"Graphic design is the lingua franca of the post-literate, global monoculture of capital, amusement, crisis, and convenience. Through sign, signal, and code (graphic design's stock in trade), our insane and insanely fragmented, yet homogenous tribe manages to cohere, just enough, to keep limping, hurling, and grinding along into an ever-more incoherent future."

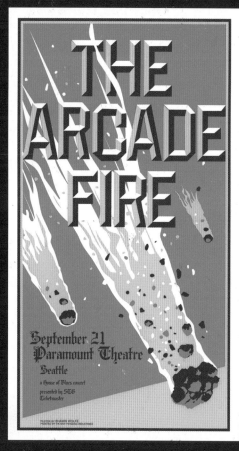

Above: I'm Alive™ poster.

Below: Arcade Fire poster.   **Right:** Bush League T-shirt.

Angus Hyland, Pentagram, London, UK

"Communicating visually by shaping the form for existing content (usually), editing or adding to existing content (sometimes) and originating both form and content (occasionally)."

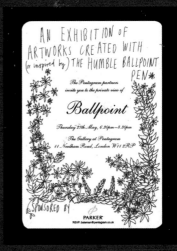

Being here: local tendencies in graphic design

In an era of globalization, increasing numbers of designers are discovering that being from somewhere in particular and designing work that feels as if it comes from somewhere in particular—rather than everywhere and, ultimately, nowhere—has never been more important.

Today's designers operate in a globally oriented economy. As globalization opens new markets, designers must often be at the vanguard, adapting a brand or product to many new cultures. The clients, collaborators, printers, programmers, and audiences that contribute to a piece of graphic design are scattered across the globe, and physical meetings between them are increasingly rare. Global-ness and the globally nomadic designer have been embraced and endorsed by contemporary design culture. The shared belief is that with a titanium laptop, wi-fi connection, and some Mandarina Duck luggage, your design practice can be as peripatetic as you are. New ideas flow in the interim zones of airport lounges and during long-haul flights that involve two ethereal sunrises. Furthermore, connecting to the concerns of people beyond one's immediate working environment is essential to the breadth of thinking that distinguishes worldly design. It is as if the design community has finally achieved the universalizing ambitions of the early 20th-century International Typography Style movement.

Many designers have welcomed their new global responsibilities. As their client base has dispersed, they've opened offices in multiple time zones, hung clocks over their reception desks set to show the current time in Shanghai, Cape Town, and Buenos Aires, and added phrases such as "global reach" to their agency descriptions. Vince Frost, for example—the consummate global designer—has design studios in London and Sydney, and is currently working with clients in London, Beijing, Dubai, and Hong Kong. He art directs the literary magazine *Zembla* from Sydney, it is published in London, and then distributed globally. "You can be anywhere in the world today and be designing," says Frost. "There was a time only a few years ago when large corporations went to large design firms in their own cities. They don't do that anymore. They've learned that smaller organizations are much more hands-on and unique in their thinking and that, thanks to good e-mail connections, it's not necessary to be in the same country as the project."

Base, a design studio, originally with its headquarters in Brussels, now has additional offices in Barcelona, New York, Madrid, and Paris. "I'm on the phone or iChat every day about jobs in different parts of the world," says Dimitri Jeurissen, partner in Base. Jeurissen pushes for seamless interchanges between the output of the five studios: "At the end of a job, you don't know who did it, because there's been input from everyone," he says. He travels extensively and what he finds on his travels feeds his work.

Jeurissen is well aware of the negative connotations of being global, however. He dislikes the fact that, "There's a certain type of shop or hotel in which you will not know what city you are in," and the Base Web site jokes that the company plans, "To open a new studio somewhere in the world every three minutes, just like McDonalds."

The danger is that if design becomes too international, accessible, and adaptable, it becomes bland and loses the specificity and local references that let you know it's actually from

THIS •••••••••••••• **sans**
IS PRI◇RI

✦ ▩ ✦ ▩ ✦ In the beginning there was the W□rd.
And the Word was **VIRUS**.

Priori Sans typeface
Designed by Jonathan Barnbrook. Prioi Sans is consciously "English" both in its form and its historical references. Priori emanates from Barnbrook's interest in British typography of the early 20th-century. It is inspired by the work of influential typographers, such as Eric Gill and Edward Johnston, and it incorporates the distilled essence of signage and lettering that Barnbrook observes in the streets, cathedrals, and public buildings of London.

someplace. Rudy Vanderlans, cofounder, publisher, and editor of *Emigre* magazine, sees the fact that so much graphic design seems created independent of its surroundings as "an impoverishment of culture." He continues, "I like it when someone wears their immediate environment on their sleeve. Today, there are so many globalization forces at work, to make everything look the same, that I think it has become the responsibility of everyone, including designers, to point out and maintain our respective cultural features. Designers can do this through their work by looking for inspiration from sources close to them."

Similarly frustrated with design that is "Generic, rootless, reductive," is designer and educator Denise Gonzales Crisp. She says, "At this very moment, design is spreading neutralizing seeds around the globe, like promiscuous missionaries. But unlike the missionary, whose beliefs we might have some insight into, the dominant design language appears to be without tenet and without politics. It is, in a word, 'globalicious'." Graphic designer, type designer, and typographer Jonathan Barnbrook sums up his feelings on the topic with the word "globanalization," and expresses this idea visually through a series of works that critique the pervasive reach of multinationals. A series of Tibetan prayer mandalas, for example, are found, on closer inspection, to have been built up from thousands of tiny corporate logos.

In the light of all this, increasing numbers of designers are discovering the importance of connecting to a place and a locality, for a sense of identity and as a source of inspiration, as a way to connect with

Left: New 42nd Street Studios identity and environmental graphics
Designed by Paula Scher, Pentagram. The graphics reflect the chaotic signage in nearby Times Square.

Below: Shakespeare in the Park promotional materials
Designed by Paula Scher, Pentagram. The promotional materials that Scher and her team have designed for the Public Theater since the mid-1990s are evocative of the dynamic tension between New York's visual and verbal noise level and its street grid.

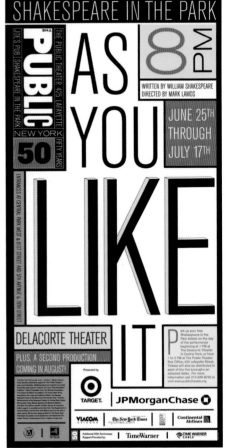

consumers who feel alienated and disconnected by their experience of globalized society. A designer like Paula Scher, partner at Pentagram, for example, describes her relationship to the city and streets of New York as being, "Intellectual, emotional, and spiritual." Her environmental graphics for the New 42nd Street Studios, a building that houses rehearsal spaces and a small theater, and her posters for the Public Theater encapsulate the visual and verbal noise level of the city, its grid layout, and the vertiginous plunge of its skyscrapers.

Similarly connected to the fabric and the noise of a city—in this case Berlin—is design studio cyan. A well-established but continually innovative force in the Berlin design community, cyan was founded in 1992 by Daniela Haufe and Detlef Fiedler and focuses almost entirely on cultural commissions. Finding creative solutions within low budgets is a consistent aspect of cyan's work, much of which demonstrates an expert handling of two-color printing, a legacy from the pre-1989 days when design was a state-controlled industry in East Berlin. Their work is vibrant, bold, and even brash, and speaks directly of their urban environment. They say they are sensitive to the ways in which the noise and chaos of the building site that surrounds them intrudes upon and influences their "inner building site." In their words, "From the material lying around in a mess, unformed, something new arises and sound is an integral part of this. Nothing was ever built silently."

The Gotham typeface, designed by Tobias Frere-Jones, was chosen for inscription into the 20-ton slab of granite in the cornerstone of the Freedom Tower, the building currently being erected on the site of the World Trade Center in New York. The choice of Gotham for such a prominent building represents the neat completion of a circle, because Gotham was inspired by the sans serif lettering found on many mid-20th century office buildings, and in the neon-lit aluminum channel letters used for liquor stores and car parks in New York. Here, it is refreshed and recontextualized on the city's most blatant symbol of civic pride. The germ of the typeface was the sign that read Port Authority Bus Terminal, and in order to find some ancillary sources that would help fill out the character set, Frere-Jones focused on the fronts of office buildings in mid-town Manhattan. "In that process, I started noticing some other stuff on the street which, while it didn't relate to Gotham at all, was worth taking a picture of." The stuff he began photographing was what he calls, "Non-typographic lettering" (he carefully avoids using the word "vernacular") and which includes hand-painted, gilt, and engraved type. His collection of photographs of signage lettering from the streets of New York currently numbers about 4,000.

From the consumer's point of view, there is also a yearning for products that are authentic and local—even if they are halfway across the globe and ultimately dislocated from place. The irony is that the more we are aware of everything that's happening everywhere, the more we want to connect with something, somewhere. Base provides the creative direction for a magazine called *BEople*, for example, which is about Belgian culture and, as such, would appear to have defined its market geographically. "Our starting point was very local," recalls Jeurissen, "but soon we were working on this subject with an international team of collaborators. Then, despite its very local cultural interest, you have people buying it in New York and Tokyo." *BEople* is just one instance of this trend in which design plays a key role.

Re-Magazine, created by Dutch designer Jop van Bennekom, is another example of this unexpected trend. Despite the specificity and locality of its content (whole issues are devoted to single individuals—the dietary habits of Marcel, a 44-year-old sales representative from Wavrin, a village on the outskirts of Lille; or Hester, a depressed woman from London), its readership is defined not by place but instead by a shared mind-set that transcends geography.

Our potential for connectedness at a transnational level, through conferences, competitions, festivals, exhibitions, visiting professorships, blogs, online and print publications, ftp sites, and text messaging, can be all-consuming and disorienting. In an effort to find focus and, ultimately, identity, readers of publications such as *BEople* or *Re-Magazine* are seeking resonances that are as local as possible, even if those localities are on the other side of the world.

Left: Freunde Guter Musik concert poster
Designed by cyan. Each event organized by the Freunde Guter Musik takes place in a different venue in Berlin, so cyan based their designs for the group on the concept of space. This poster shows a space with what cyan call "an almost cosy living room atmosphere."

Above: Singuhr poster
Designed by cyan. The Parochial Church in Berlin, nicknamed "Singuhr," is now used for sound/music projects. The theme for this festival was the creation of invisible but perceptible soundspaces. By overprinting the various moirees cyan created "some kind of sound cluster, similar to the one that arises in and around each visitor's head."

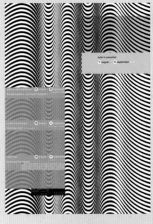

Above: Singuhr posters
Designed by cyan. **Main picture:** this poster establishes the new "Singuhr" location by using a cock (crowing for attention) and a ventilator (bringing fresh air into the old church, but also resembling a

clock). The theme for the events was "resonances" so cyan put three regular waves on top of each other.
Top: This poster for the "Suite in Parochial" sound art festival was silkscreen printed in fluorescent green, gold, and

black, representing an attempt to put what the designers call "the spherical aspect and the punctual impulses into a rigorous eye-catching form."
Bottom: The concept for this season of music at the Parochial church explored

the use of jazz in the realm of sound installations. cyan responded by designing a "pure" type-based black and white poster.

Gotham typeface (above) and New York street signage (left)
Design and photographs by Tobias Frere-Jones, Hoefler & Frere Jones type foundry. Inspired by the lettering found on utilitarian buildings in New York, Gotham is inscribed into the slab of granite in the cornerstone of the Freedom Tower, the building currently being erected on the site of the World Trade Center.

Re-Magazine [12]
Hester

DEPRESSED

Left and below: "Hester"
and "Marcel" issues
of *Re-Magazine*
Designed and published by
Jop van Bennekom.

Re-Magazine [11]
Marcel

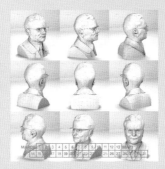

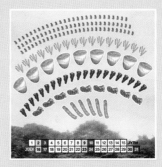

Publikum calendar
Designed by karlssonwilker.
Hjalti Karlsson and Jan Wilker,
of karlssonwilker, were invited
to design a calendar for a
Serbian organization called
Publikum. They agreed to do
it on the condition that they
would spend 12 days in
Serbia, producing one
calendar page per day in
response to what they saw,
heard, experienced, and ate.
They visited the monuments of
the former communist regime
and the ruins remaining from
the 1999 NATO bombing in
Yugoslavia. They also went to
traditional taverns, visited
markets, and "inhaled the feel
for everyday life of ordinary
people in Serbia."

Andrew Ashton
Studio Pip and Co., Victoria,
Australia

"From what I can see, graphic design exists to express ideas. For example: A person has an idea for an organic juice bar; the graphic design gives the bar a presence and distinguishes it from the businesses that surround it. An organization or individual has a wonderful garden to share with the public; the graphic design is the signing that helps all to enjoy and explore the facility as the organization or individual intended. A public issue arises that needs urgent attention; the graphic design is the poster campaign or the free newspaper strategically placed in the public domain. These examples represent possibly millions of such ideas.

"Graphic design helps people to distinguish ideas, make choices, enjoy ideas, orient themselves in the day to day. It so happens graphic design can also create an enormous amount of pleasure and satisfaction in those who generate it. Activities such as graphic design are expressions that indicate the diversity and richness of any given culture.

"Graphic design is the supposed personality or face of an idea. However, effective graphic design is the outcome that touches a desired audience with economy and yet leaves one with the idea rather than the graphic design itself.

"Marketing people think that graphic design is a function of marketing; graphic designers liken graphic design to art; historians see graphic design as social ephemera. I see it as one of those fascinating traits of being human."

James Victore
James Victore Inc,
New York, US

Cross-disciplinary design and collaboration

Graphic design is becoming increasingly interdisciplinary, geographically distributed, and collaborative. Complex problems require sophisticated responses that draw from expertise in multiple fields. When various disciplines converge or collide, all kinds of new challenges can arise: how to organize large amorphous and globally dispersed teams; how to communicate with one another; how to determine who does what; how to make discipline-specific technologies sync up, and so on.

You no longer have to be a big firm to compete for large or multidisciplinary jobs. Smaller design firms can respond to complex multichannel projects by quickly expanding and enlisting the expertise of collaborators from other disciplines. Open, a small firm in New York, took on the recent rebranding of the Bravo television network. The call came in October 2004 when Open consisted of four people: the studio's founder and principal Scott Stowell, another designer, a production manager, and an intern. The project had to be completed by January 1, 2005, so Stowell quickly assembled a team for the project that included six designers, 12 animators, 10 illustrators, a music producer, and a producer.

Open decided to use the metaphor of a magazine as the "driving engine" for the network's identity. They designed graphic sequences for each program that were, in Stowell's words, "Like a printed magazine page, exploded." All the elements of a magazine, such as headlines, letters to the editor, reviews, spot illustrations, rules, and columns of text found their direct counterparts in the screen version. Lauren Zalaznick, the president of Bravo and Trio, asked Stowell to try it in 3D. "This was a much better solution," says Stowell. "Now the viewer feels as if they are moving through the physical space of a magazine." Once the initial concepts were approved, Stowell and his team had to move fast to make the deadline. They had to direct live action and still photography shoots in New York and Los Angeles, write everything, and then commission illustrations, animation, design, music, and voice-over.

To make the project work, Stowell had to step back, give people parameters, and see what would happen. "My whole day would be taken up making just one round of all the people working on the project, seeing what they were doing, giving notes, and then it would be time to start all over again." Most of the collaborators worked out of house. Agoraphone produced the music from a separate office, and for the live action shoots, Open hired a production company, a director, and a prop-making group. Animators, too, all worked from home. "All the technology they need," says Stowell, "Is a G5 with a big screen and lots of RAM, and a beer holder."

In fact, technology is one of the key factors in this kind of endeavor. Adobe After Effects, in particular, played a big part in enabling a small outfit like Open to take on such a considerable project. "Years ago when I did motion graphics at M&Co," says Stowell, "We were pasting things up, and to move a piece of type on a big machine would take six hours. Then we would do it in Illustrator and take it to a facility, where they would make it in After Effects, but we would be directing them and they would be a separate company.

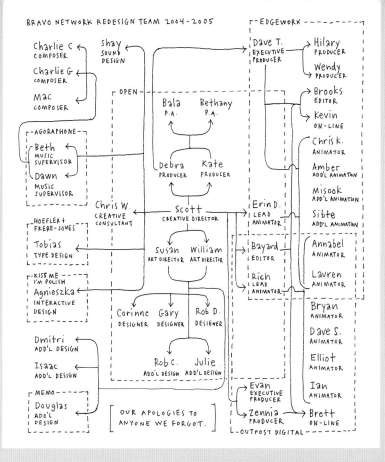

Bravo logo and stills (below) and diagram of the design team (left) Designed by Open. This redesign for the Bravo network was intended to evoke the experience of being in a 3D magazine. Open had to expand their design team to complete the project on time.

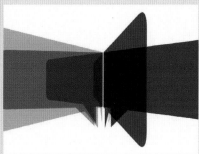

Bloomberg headquarters environmental graphics
Designed by Paula Scher and Lisa Strausfeld, Pentagram. Working with Studios

Architecture, Pentagram designed an interior that communicates Bloomberg's brand and services—data, news, and information.

Now, all of them have become designers and all designers have become production artists. It's all merging together in a way that's both exciting and disturbing to me."

When the designers had completed the designs for frames, those frames would need to be approved by Bravo. To facilitate such a frequency and depth of communication, they used a Web-based project management tool for presentations. The online tool works like a blog. Every link represents a presentation. Every presentation consists of many files, such as QuickTimes, PDFs, and sound files. Clients would add their feedback and designers would resubmit revised versions. Open's other primary form of communication with collaborators, both inside and outside the office, is Instant Messaging. Says Stowell, "The file transfers you can do are so much better than e-mail or FTP because people can send me a 30MB file in 30 seconds."

Of course, working collaboratively within and beyond design is not a radical new concept. Pentagram, possibly design's most respected and well-known firm, was set up in 1972 to accommodate scenarios of collaborative interactive practice. Ever since, the international 19-partner firm has represented multiple disciplines and collaboration has been integral to its ethos. When the financial news, data, and analytics provider Bloomberg approached Pentagram to create environmental graphics for its multiple-floor corporate headquarters in New York, Paula Scher, a partner with signage design expertise, and Lisa Strausfeld, a partner with interactive design expertise, worked together on the project along with

Studios Architecture. "Because the project involved both building graphics and media installations, it was a natural opportunity for collaboration," says Strausfeld. "Paula and I were both up for the challenge and also happen to share an interest in 'information art'." Together, the partners created a vibrant environment that seamlessly integrates information into its functionality. It includes identification signage for floors, rooms, and elevators, directory signage and wayfinding, and several dynamic, superscale media installations. Numbers, the raw material of all Bloomberg's transactions, are at the core of all the elements of the design. Staggered strips of LED screens display a continual feed of news, weather, and market data extracted from Bloomberg's live coverage. The floors are marked with translucent, color-coded resin numbers encased in glass.

Similarly, Strausfeld's design of a Web site for Mohawk Paper Mills is built on collaborative foundations. "Collaboration describes the working process of everything I do at Pentagram—collaboration with clients, members of my team, and, of course, my other partners," says Strausfeld. Once Strausfeld and her team had established a concept for the site—they wanted it to reflect as much as possible the physical properties of paper and the way one shuffles piles or loose leaves of paper around a desk—they began to make studies of various paper behaviors as a way to map out potential interactions.

"Collaboration is different from design-by-committee," Strausfeld points out. "Successful design collaborations yield singular, coherent, and rigorous design solutions. Everyone has to be on board with a single concept." In the case of the Mohawk Web site, everyone on the team worked to develop an interaction model that abstractly referred to paper. Intern Josh Nimoy did the motion studies for animations of crumpled balls of paper that flatten out to reveal their surfaces. Team member Tamara Maletic created studies of the ways in which paper gracefully spills and scatters from piles and, choreographing the suite as a whole, Jack Zerby looked at series of behaviors to find ways of defining different sections of the site, through variations in paper rhythm, movement, and placement, translated into staggers, slips, rows, and fans. Designer-client collaboration was also crucial to the success of this project. Strausfeld points to the fact that she and her client, Laura Shore, could have direct dialog, and that Shore could sign off on designs without having to run them through various committees, as one of the reasons for the project's integrity.

Many new designers are undeterred by the concept of working as a large team and wearing multiple creative hats in any one day. They belong to a new generation who are not used to boundaries between areas of creative practice. Increasingly, design colleges are introducing transdisciplinary courses both to prepare students for the new realities of the workplace and to reflect their natural tendencies.·

At the Art Center College of Design in Pasadena, California, for example, MA students from various design backgrounds pool their areas of expertise in the Transdisciplinary Studio. Run by product design instructor Karen Hofman, graphic

design department chair Nikolaus Hafermaas, and the science fiction writer and Art Center's current "Visionary in Residence," Bruce Sterling, the focus is on working as a team on all aspects of a design project from conceptualization to product promotion.

The 2005 INDEX Future Scenarios was a recent collaborative project in which 14 Art Center students from five departments (Graphic Design, Environmental Design, Photography and Imaging, Product Design, and Graduate Media) relocated for several weeks to Copenhagen to create an exhibition for the annual INDEX Design And Innovation Awards. The students were charged with the art direction, design, and production of the exhibition and exterior design for nine pavilions, as well as the exhibition identity and storefront teasers throughout the main shopping streets of Copenhagen. For the curation of the exhibition, Art Center students collaborated with those at seven other design schools from around the world. Working together via Web platforms and conventional mail, the students were required to produce design solutions for the year 2010 in the areas of Body, Work, Home, Play, and Community. In Hafermaas' opinion, the project enables students to, "Practice the interplay of graphic design, product design, imaging, motion, and environmental design," and at the same time, "Learn to globally communicate and cooperate."

The MA course in Design Studies at Central Saint Martin's in London was launched in 1991 to provide an alternative to what course leader Geoff Cook saw as, "The somewhat limited scope of educational and professional approaches to design."

The degree program attracts students from all areas of the design industry, along with marketers, managers, and entrepreneurs who would like to develop their creative skills. Cook believes that an interdisciplinary approach produces lateral-thinking designers, who are sensitive to the skills and experience of noncreative as well as creative people.

Throughout the course, students work on a number of team projects. Can You Design a Trend? is an example of a two-week assignment, whereby the class has to work in teams to research, invent, and present a trend within the industry, making the intangible tangible. Projects such as this emphasize, as Cook puts it, "The value of process not just product," and teach students to broaden their understanding of the industry as a whole.

Designers and forward-thinking companies are just waking up to the benefits of this kind of unconventional approach. As Design Studies graduate, Tyler Mallison, says, "By involving people that have a broad understanding and empathy for many areas, along with a deep expertise in one or two areas, new perspectives can be achieved."

Mohawk Paper Mills
Web site
Designed by Lisa Strausfeld, Pentagram. The site design is intended to reflect the physical properties of paper.

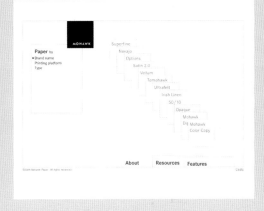

**"INDEX Design And
Innovation Awards"
exhibition design**
Students from five departments
from the Art Center College
of Design, Pasadena,
collaborated with one another
and students from seven other
design schools to curate and
design an exhibition about life
in the year 2010 for the 2005
INDEX Design And Innovation
Awards in Copenhagen.

Dana Arnett
VSA Partners, Chicago, US

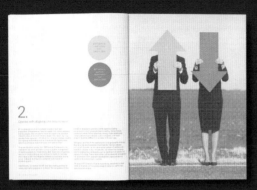

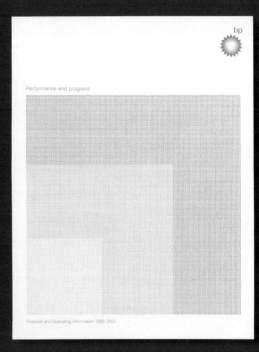

"In pondering the response to this question, my mind sadly detours to the comedy of Jeff Foxworthy. For those of you who are not familiar with his staple routine, I'll attempt to recall an example of his patented blue-collar humor:

'If you attend the family reunion in search of a date, you just may be a redneck.'

"Foxworthy's use of rhetorical humor strikes me as a means of addressing the query at play in this book. Allow me to demonstrate:

'If you automatically brake when you see a stop sign, you just may know what graphic design is for.'
or
'If you voted for George Bush when you thought you had voted for Al Gore, you just may know what graphic design is for.'
or
'If shortly after the events of 9/11, you were inspired to wear your "I love NYC" T-shirt, you just may know what graphic design is for.'

"As illustrated, design in the graphic form can create order out of chaos, decide an election, and (most notably) inspire us to stand up for things that are near and dear to us.

"Rationally speaking, graphic design plays on countless levels—its very power and purpose spans a broad spectrum of possibilities. It can invisibly skim the surface or go a level deeper. And, thankfully, design isn't required to make a choice between form or function—it can be a vehicle for both. Perhaps seminal American graphic designer Paul Rand said it best, 'Graphic design provides a context for understanding.' For now, I'll defer to 'his late majesty's' definition. Rand hasn't sold millions of records like Mr. Foxworthy, but his designs and teachings have inspired countless admirers to answer this question for ourselves."

Deborah Adler
Milton Glaser Inc.
New York, US

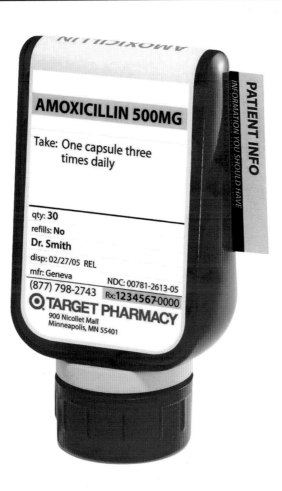

"For the designer, it's an endless process of exploring, learning and working which forms a vehicle to communicate. For the community, graphic design makes it easier for people to understand information. It is purposeful and has intention. It also has the possibility to connect people."

Designer as author, publisher, producer, curator, entrepreneur

No longer content to execute other people's projects, many graphic designers are seizing control of their work by creating, marketing, and selling their own products. Today, many designers are their own clients, their own agents. They set up their own clothing and music labels, furniture and product lines, they open galleries, publish magazines, moderate blogs, and organize events. What is valued more than specialization is ambidextrous exchange, both among the activities close to design—such as art, illustration, motion, type, fashion, product, and writing—and those further afield—such as editing, curating, and inventing. The reasons for such fluidity are various—for some, it's about authorship, for some it's about entrepreneurship. For most, however, it's about a widely felt dissatisfaction with the models and forums currently available for the production and presentation of graphic designers' work. By embracing the potential to generate new ideas and make them happen, designers are able to change the status quo directly and meaningfully.

The term "authorship" has been used in connection with design since the 1990s when it was first introduced as a way of referring to the expansion of design's agency. To Katherine McCoy, it is closely connected to literary authorship. In 1990, when she was director of 2D Design at Cranbrook Academy of Art, Michigan, McCoy wrote a piece titled "American Graphic Design Expression" for *Design Quarterly*, in which she discussed designers who were dissatisfied with the obedient delivery of the client's message and who were going beyond "the problem solving tradition," to investigate the role of, "interpreter." Referring, in large part, to the students and teachers associated with Cranbrook at that time—Ed Fella, Lorraine Wild, Jeffrey Keedy, Andrew Blauvelt, and Allen Hori, among them—she invoked the term "author" very specifically, for its literary resonance: "By authoring additional content and a self-conscious critique of the message, they are adopting roles associated with both art and literature."

Michael Rock defined these terms more broadly in an article published in *Eye* magazine in 1996. He talks about literature as a model for design, but also about filmmaking, artists' books, activism, and other methods for establishing "authority" over production. In Rock's opinion, a designer is an author only when their work contains sustained evidence of "technical proficiency," "stylistic consistency," and "interior meaning." He cites only a handful of designers whose work bears up to such scrutiny—Jan van Toorn, Vaughan Oliver, Anthon Beeke, and Ed Fella. He also turns his attention in the article to those designers who write, edit, and publish, and singles out Abbott Miller and Ellen Lupton as designers who, through their innovative writing and exhibitions, have constructed a new approach to graphic design, coupled with an exploratory practice.

Other designers see in authorship an opportunity and an inspiration for design to have more of a presence well beyond the design realm—a rationalization for design's place at the high table, where the important decisions are made concerning global affairs. The activities and pronouncements of Canadian designer Bruce Mau's studio in the past few years represent the most

"Free Library" exhibition
Curated by Mark Owens of
Life of the Mind.

exaggerated example of design's new imperialistic tendencies. The Institute Without Boundaries, a joint initiative of Mau's studio and the School of Design at George Brown Toronto City College, is a one-year interdisciplinary postgraduate design program that aims to produce a new breed of designer—one who is, in the words of Buckminster Fuller, a synthesis of artist, inventor, mechanic, objective economist, and evolutionary strategist. Massive Change: The Future of Global Design is the suitably bombastic sounding title of the students' inaugural project. Massive Change looks in detail at global issues such as energy resources, urbanization, and military spending, and locates design firmly at the center of their solutions.

The MFA program of the School of Visual Arts, New York, which is called Designer As Author, equates authorship with entrepreneurship. SVA MFA student theses are products that are formulated or fabricated as viable commercial concepts with specific audiences in mind. They include things like a model for a future design school in India, a line of clocks for people who don't care what time it is, and a collection of home furnishings created from obsolete technologies. The students develop business plans, conduct market research, and study intellectual property law. Deborah Adler (see page 33) is a recent graduate whose thesis project is a labeling system for medications that is clear and easy to read—so clear and easy to read, in fact, that retailer Target is putting it into production, and it was selected by MoMA for display in a major design exhibition about design's responses to danger and risk. She was inspired to make this product after her grandmother took her husband's prescriptions by mistake because the type used was so small. Such a project truly encapsulates the goal of the program, to: "Extend beyond the traditional definitions of graphic design into the realm of concept creat[ion] and product[ion]."

Elsewhere, many designers have started ancillary enterprises such as a gallery space, a store, a blog, a publication, or a series of design lectures. Others spend time writing, photographing, or directing. None of these activities is treated as tangential or a hobby; instead, in an increasingly competitive industry, they become the defining, passion-fueled characteristics of a design firm—the most effective form of calling cards.

British designer Stuart Bailey and Slovakian designer Peter Bilak decided to edit and publish a publication about visual culture. "The idea was to forge a new kind of approach to writing, less overtly historical or theoretical, largely written by graphic designers themselves, rather than historians or theorists, with a healthy disregard for journalistic conventions," says Bailey. They launched Dot Dot Dot in 2000 with minimal means—some money they made from teaching a workshop and the support of a generous printer. After that, "It was always a patching together of sales and advertising money, with occasional contributions from Dutch art funding," says Bailey. At first, production and distribution were a real challenge: "Printers having to reprint, then missing shipments and holding onto boxes of thousands of copies for months without telling anyone they hadn't been collected."

Dot Dot Dot magazine covers and spreads
Edited, designed, and published by Stuart Bailey and Peter Bilak. The magazine is built on inventive critical writing about the undervalued and overlooked aspects—the B-sides and outtakes—of graphic design practice and thinking.

F7 postcards
Designed by deValence.
These postcards are to
promote the lecture series
deValence directs and hosts
as part of the collective, F7.

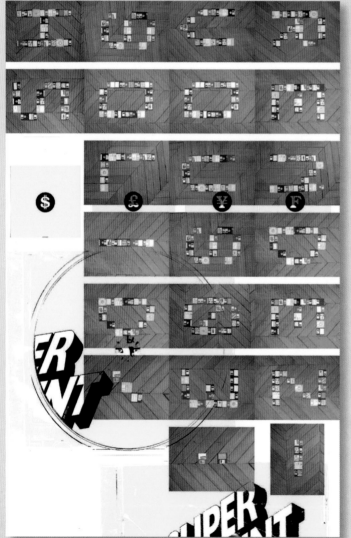

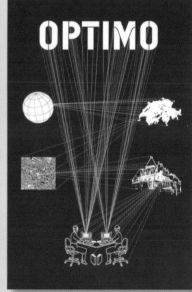

Right: Green Lady T-shirts
Designed and produced by
Gary Benzel and Todd St. John,
Green Lady.

The realities of being their own clients on a project that had to be done in their spare time soon became starkly apparent to the designers. "It was our after-hours-ness, in combination with bad luck, bad distributors, and bad shops," says Bailey. Ten issues later, when the magazine was a critical success and being distributed by Central in London and Princeton Architectural Press in the US, Bailey and Bilak were able to leave their enthusiastic, but nonpaying, distributor Actar.

Despite the theoretical success, but financial tenuousness of the magazine, Bailey says he doesn't have any doubt that he'll carry on. The magazine's creators enjoy making a virtue of necessity. Their response to a current cash flow problem, for example, is to, "Use [the opportunity] to strip down to black and white. We're becoming the Ramones again," says Bailey. "In the end, it'll always get done while the impetus is there. It could be a few sheets of paper and it would be fine if the content is there."

The design of the magazine feeds from the world of fanzines and ad-hoc printing, and the intention is to produce something that feels under- or un-designed, as if the articles had come through on a fax machine, been annotated, and then incorporated directly into the body of the magazine. Of course, the very fact that designers—and very thoughtful ones, at that—are at the helm of such a process makes it impossible for them to produce something wholly un-designed, but it's the tension between order and chaos, control and chance that give this visual culture document its palpable vitality and integrity.

Mark Owens, a *Dot Dot Dot* contributor and freelance designer, has recently curated an exhibition called "The Free Library" that juxtaposes the work of designers and artists whose work engages with language, writing, and books. Most of the participants are self-publishers whose output takes the form of writing, silk-screens, zines, stickers, and other forms that Owens describes as offering an "accessible, free platform for ideas." The traveling show, that takes the form of a reading room, began at The Riviera, a gallery space in Brooklyn, which was co-founded by Mark's brother, Matt Owens.

Increasing numbers of designers, frustrated with the inadequacies of so many design publishers who purport to value design, but don't invest the care and resources necessary to make beautiful and

Wood-grain pattern wallet, magazine rack, and cushion
Designed and produced by Gary Benzel and Todd St. John, HunterGatherer.

enduring books, are establishing their own imprints. Winterhouse Editions in the US, run by designers and Design Observer blog co-founders William Drentell and Jessica Helfand, publishes literary works, books on design, and cultural criticism. Every aspect of the books' production is well considered and overseen directly by the designers. In the interest of stimulating: "Public and critical discourse about the course of our society's future," Helfand and Drentell were also responsible for the printing of a policy paper that outlines the US government's national security strategy.

Many designers, then, are repositioning their activities at the source rather than at the production end of a project as a way to assert control over the content of their work and conditions in which they do it. Increased control brings with it increased responsibility, of course, but the thrill (and sometimes fear) of generating your own idea, and then producing it and selling it to your own specifications, tends to motivate one to overcome the trickiest of obstacles. The design firm Browns publishes books about design that showcase the work of their collaborators—such as the photographer Robin Broadbent and the illustrator Paul Davis. "In busy studio life, the books keep us sane and allow us the chance to define ourselves as designers on a more personal level," says Jonathan Ellery, partner at Browns. "The books I choose to work on tend to come from relationships that I have with photographers, artists, writers, musicians, composers, fashion designers, and printers. In fact, anything that I find interesting or, rather selfishly, can turn into an adventure."

Graphic designers do not confine their entrepreneurial activities to traditional graphic design products such as books and magazines, though. The realms of product, fashion, and art are also fair game. In 1994, Todd St. John, designer, animator, and filmmaker, initiated Green Lady, a clothing and product line, in collaboration with designer Gary Benzel. They continue to make and sell a range of products—such as T-shirts, cushions, skateboards, bags, and even a collapsible table—that are sold online and in outlets including Benzel's San Diego store, Igloo. One of the ideas behind the products is that they are compact and portable and therefore suitable for a contemporary nomadic lifestyle.

HunterGatherer is the mental space and physical workshop through which St. John works on client-based design projects, including many motion design projects for companies such as MTV. Ideas and themes flow between the self-initiated and the client-driven projects, but St. John makes an effort to keep them as separate entities and to redress the balance if it feels as if one is dominating at any one time.

In a similar vein, Agathe Jacquillat and Tomi Vollauschek who run FL@33, a visual communications studio based in London, also oversee stereohype.com, an online boutique of limited editions that reference fashion and graphic art. Ever since they established the firm in 2001, they have put a special emphasis on self-initiated projects such as a magazine called *trans-form*, and an online collection of sounds called bzzzpeek.com, which they feel tend to inform their commissioned work in healthy ways. The projects also have the advantage of bringing FL@33 into contact with publishers and other designers around the world. "It was really a logical next step to launch our online graphic art and fashion boutique," say the designers. "Stereohype allows us to design and produce our own clothing range and artworks and sell T-shirts, magazines, prints, and posters to a global audience."

Such designers, whether working with the currency of ideas or of things, are developing a vibrant network of creative workshops in which there are no divisions between directing and producing, thinking and making. Because they are in control of the conditions of making, not only can they create new products and ideas, they can also devise new economies for creative practice and reset the standards for quality in ways that will ultimately have impact on more established—and more complacent—institutions and companies.

Butterfly sculpture contains 938 pencils
© 2002 FL@33
agathe jacquillat + tomi vollauschek
www.flat33.com

Stereohype
graphic art and fashion boutique
www.stereohype.com

ε3

**Butterfly artwork, toy,
Stereohype logo and label**
Designed by FL@33 and sold
through their online boutique,
Stereohype.

Button badges
Various designers. Made for
a FL@33 project that had
the brief to create "a massive
collection of wearable one-
inch canvases."

Alan Fletcher, London, UK

"Earning a bob or two."

Menagerie of Imaginary Creatures: Conceived to amuse my three-year-old grandson. The creatures were constructed from wine corks, flip-top cigarette packs, toilet roll cores, bottle caps, ice-cream paddles, drawing pins, film cassettes, plastic spoons, newspapers, flour and water, watercolors, varnish and lots of patience.

Daniel Eatock
Eatock Ltd., London, UK

ABCDEFGHIJKLMNOPQRSTUVWXYZ

my favourite cup

Email

Junk Mail

This postcard is temporarily out of stock

PRIVATE AND CONFIDENTIAL

Design for protest

Graphic design gives a visual voice to the social and political concerns of the day. There is a rich legacy of design for dissent and protest from which today's politically motivated designers can draw. With the Internet, there is also an important new vehicle for distributing materials and organizing resistance. The current political climate has inspired many designers to put their time and talents behind the causes they believe in, and explore new messages and methods.

At one end of the spectrum are graphic activists making aggressive statements in the streets. Robbie Conal, for example, is a Los Angeles-based artist who regularly makes acerbic caricatures of political figures that are disseminated guerrilla-style by groups of volunteers who meet at midnight with buckets of wheatpaste glue. Conal says he uses these "Art Attacks" to: "Communicate directly to regular people on the street versus a mediated form of distribution, like showing in art galleries…" James Victore, a self-taught illustrator, designer and artist, based in New York, regularly produces and publishes his own posters that provide caustic graphic social critique. The posters are produced in small editions but their regular display and reproduction, and the fact they are collected by museums such as the Library of Congress in Washington DC, increase their power and influence.

Such designers belong to a long and active tradition of graphic protest. In the early 1930s, John Heartfield used the compositional strategy of montage to create satirical commentaries on the politics of Weimar Germany. His biting portrayals of Hitler being fed by capitalist funding and Goering as responsible for the Reichstag fire were published in *AIZ*, a communist photo newspaper. In fragmenting and recomposing images found in the press, Heartfield commented on media constructions of reality—a critique that began during the Dada period and continues to this day.

The student protests of the late 1960s were accompanied by posters made by idealistic art collectives. In France, one of these collectives developed into Grapus, the members of which would spend the next 20 years producing spirited posters for communist causes.

Ken Garland is a key figure in the history of politically motivated design. In 1964 he published a manifesto entitled "First Things First," signed by 21 other designers and photographers, that asked for a refocusing of design's attention and energies away from consumer advertising and toward social causes.

At first glance, the tools for dissent at graphic design's disposal may seem limited—button badges, T-shirts, posters, and magazines—and yet when generated with passion, conceived with thoughtfulness, and used effectively, such tokens can actually reach more people than their modest forms suggest. The designer Milton Glaser, alarmed by such social issues as the political exploitation of the fear of international terrorism, has decided to "become more active in civic life." In a speech at AIGA's 2005 national conference, he said, "As designers, we've been concerned about our role in society for a very long time. It's important to remember that even modernism had social reform as its basic principle, but the need to

The Death Penalty Mocks Justice

The United States remains the only Western industrialized nation to retain the death penalty and carry out executions. While the rest of the world turns its back on state sanctioned killing, the death penalty in the U.S. continues to be applied in a racist and arbitrary manner. Capital punishment has never been implemented in a fair and non-discriminatory way. It has never been proven to be a deterrent, yet our nation's death row, and executions continue to escalate. The death penalty is a mockery of justice. In the pursuit of equality before the law it must be abolished.

Political posters
Designed by James Victore. Victore's work exploits the power of visual clichés—which he subverts and customizes—to make easily understood political statements.

Shown here are "Death Penalty Mocks Justice," a poster for the National Association for the Advancement of Colored People; "Just Say No," a self-published poster protesting the Disneyfication of Times Square; and "Use a Condom."

ALDERMASTON TO LONDON EASTER 62

| Aldermaston Good Friday 12noon | Reading Easter Saturday 9am | Slough Easter Sunday 9.30am | Acton Green Easter Monday 9.30am | Hammersmith | Kensington |

RALLY HYDE PARK [near Hyde Pk Corner] **12.30–3PM**
FINAL MARCH : | Hyde Pk Corner | Sloane St | Victoria St | Whitehall |

act [today] seems more important than ever." Glaser promotes the ideals of citizenship in a positive way and advances the causes he supports through judicious use of available channels. Soon after 9/11, Glaser revised his original 1976 "I heart New York" marque by blackening one corner of the heart symbol and adding the words "more than ever." In order to broadcast the poster, Glaser turned to the *Daily News* columnist, Pete Hamill. His poster was duly wrapped around 700,000 copies of the newspaper and delivered to all the newsagents in New York who put it up in their windows and doors. Before long, the image became as ubiquitous as its predecessor. When Glaser wanted to remind people of Africa's plight, he designed a poster that was produced and distributed though the School of Visual Arts, New York, where he is a member of faculty. The telephone kiosk advertising company voluntarily tripled the number of locations

that the school had paid for, with the result that the campaign was highly visible throughout New York while the UN World Summit was in session. To Glaser, what is just as important as the actual design of personal interventions, is how to make sure people see them, or, as he said in a lecture at the 2005 AIGA conference: "How to enter into the bloodstream of the culture."

Another designer who understands the power of the media and harnesses it to gain coverage for social causes is Natalie Jeremijenko. Trained as an engineer, but equally at home in the realms of art and design, Jeremijenko has developed a number of projects that she describes as "mediagenic events." They are designed to be performance spectacles that will be witnessed by various audiences. Her Feral Robots project, for example, involves roving packs of open-source robot dogs that are released to investigate contaminated urban

Left: CND poster
Designed by Ken Garland
in 1962 for the Campaign for
Nuclear Disarmament to
promote a protest march.

**Below: Suited for
Subversion suit**
Designed by Ralph Borland.
This suit for protesters is made
from nylon-reinforced PVC,
and inflates when the protestor
feels threatened.

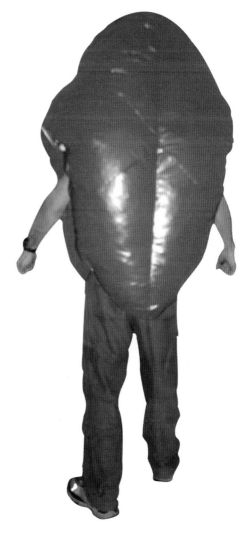

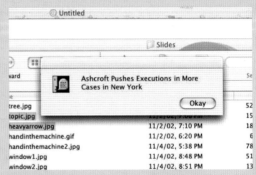

Above: Okay News
Created by Rebecca Ross.
Exploits the computer's
potential as a tool for creating
social awareness. A warning
box appears every 20 minutes,
freezing your computer and
displaying a headline from
the *New York Times*.

**Below: www.scheisse.de
billboard poster**
Designed by Uwe Loesch.
This poster was intended to
counter propaganda posted
by neo-fascists on
Mönchengladbach's official
town Web site.

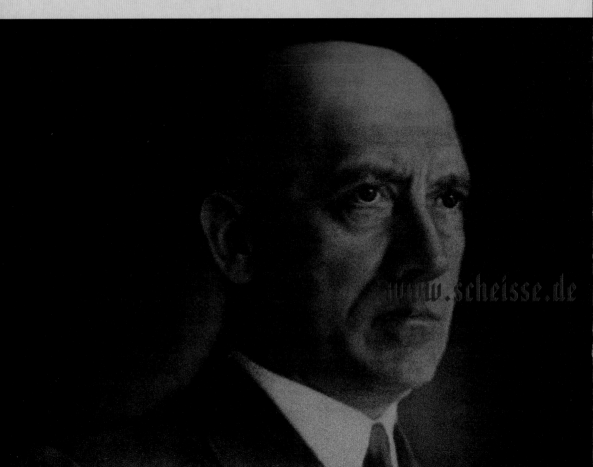

sites. The dogs began as commercially available robotic dog toys, the least expensive and most widely distributed robotic platform. The behavior of the dogs is modified with new abilities allowing them to sense an environmental toxin, to follow concentration gradients of that toxin, and to display information with their movement. Using the movements of the dogs to visualize information makes them accessible to a wider audience, including young children. The dogs go some way towards locating toxicity in the places children play, but the media attention that the project generates is arguably more important than the data itself.

In a similar vein is Suited For Subversion, the ingenious invention of South African interactive designer Ralph Borland. It's a suit for a protester to wear that inflates when he or she is threatened. The suit is fitted with a camera to document any encounters with the police and a speaker that amplifies the heartbeat to remind the police of their humanity. When gathered in a crowd with other suits, the simultaneous beating of the protester's hearts creates a dramatic and powerful rhythm.

Bikes Against Bush is an interactive protest/performance that occurred on the streets of New York during the Republican National Convention in 2004. Using a wireless Internet-enabled bicycle outfitted with a mechanical printing device, the bicycle was equipped to spray-print text messages sent from Web users directly onto the streets and sidewalks of Manhattan in water-soluble chalk. When a message was printed (in dot matrix font), www.bikesagainstbush.com

automatically updated a live map marking the location of the message. The webcam on the bike also documented this with a snapshot of the printed message. Networked technology not only fed the messages that Kinberg wrote onto the streets, but also the Web site he created for the project was quickly picked up by bloggers. The news spread to the mainstream media and "Bikes Against Bush" has been featured by Air America, Wired, CNN, The Village Voice, MSNBC, Reuters, Associated Press, and MTV.

The Internet plays a huge role in the ways in which designers are able to support the causes they believe in and create effective forms of protest. In its simplest form, the Internet is an effective and cheap method of distribution. Posters and stencils can be downloaded from anyone's computers and printed out on regular printers. This is how Shepard Fairey achieved such ubiquity with his Andre The Giant image (he even included instructions for making wheatpaste glue).

The interactive design firm Flat sends out viral digital public service announcements (PSAs) on topics such as recycling, voting, and light pollution. They use interactive technology to provide more information—and a different quality of information—than it is possible to put on printed posters. The animated PSAs, inspired by what the designers call "a Black Panthers esthetic," are built in Flash and provide multiple links through which the user can further explore the topic at hand.

Another project that exploits the computer's potential as a tool for creating social awareness is Okay News, created by designer Rebecca Ross. Once the application is installed, an operating system warning box appears every 20 minutes, freezing your computer and displaying a headline from that day's *New York Times*. The headline might say "Suicide Blast Rocks Jerusalem, Leaving Up To 40 Wounded," or "African Food For Africa's Starving is Roadblocked in Congress," and, to continue what you were doing, you have to press the Okay button. The project provides both commentary on the apathetic nature of our society as a whole, as well as drawing attention to the individual's culpability.

Perhaps the most common form of protest is invisible. By turning down projects or refusing to engage in behavior they consider unethical, designers assert their creative agency and help to educate their clients. This form of protest is difficult to document because its success results in absence—mistakes not made, paper not used, effort not wasted. This everyday form of protest is perhaps the purest because it is unlikely to be recognized—awards are not bestowed on work that is not done. Yet, refusing to do bad can be a powerful force for good.

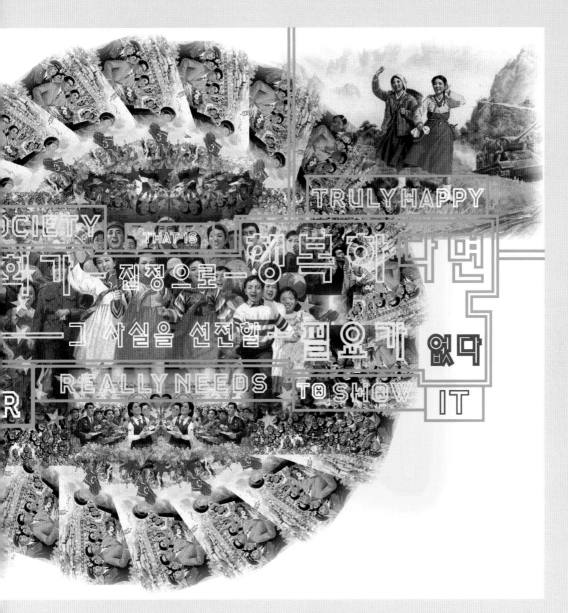

"A Society That is Truly Happy Never Really Needs to Show it" poster
Designed by Jonathan Barnbrook, in response to North Korean propaganda paintings. This and other works in a series about North Korea's recent nuclear policy, dictatorship, and the north-south division were exhibited in Seoul in 2004.

Jonathan Ellery, Browns, London, UK

"I have no idea what graphic design as a descriptor means anymore. The area it once clearly inhabited has now become so blurred with other disciplines that a whole new world has opened up. This era of continued ambiguity suits me down to the ground."

Muhammad Ali

★★★
Madison Square Garden
New York City
September 1974

Designed by Jonathan Ellery
Limited edition of thirty
Henry Peacock Gallery
London 2004

I DONE WRASSLED WITH AN ALLIGATOR, I DONE TUSSLED WITH A WHALE, I DONE HANDCUFFED LIGHTNING, THROWN THUNDER IN JAIL, THAT'S BAD. ONLY LAST WEEK I MURDERED A ROCK, INJURED A STONE, HOSPITALIZED A BRICK, I'M SO MEAN I MAKE MEDICINE SICK.

Above: 136 Points of Reference
Examines the influences that have informed and defined Ellery's and his studio's work.

Left: I Done Wrassled With...
Printed gold foil onto three materials. "Public Address System" show. Henry Peacock Gallery, London.

SCHEDULE C (Form 1040)	**Profit or Loss From Business** (Sole Proprietorship)	OMB No. 1545-0074
Department of the Treasury Internal Revenue Service	▶ Partnerships, joint ventures, etc., must file Form 1065 or 1065-B. ▶ Attach to Form 1040 or 1041. ▶ See Instructions for Schedule C (Form 1040).	2004 Attachment Sequence No. 09

Name of proprietor
BARBARA A DEWILDE

Social security number (SSN)

A	Principal business or profession, including product or service (see page C-2 of the instructions)	B Enter code from pages C-7, 8, & 9
	Graphic Designer	▶ 8 1 2 9 9 0
C	Business name. If no separate business name, leave blank.	D Employer ID number (EIN), if any

E   Business address (including suite or room no.) ▶ 361 N. FULLERTON AVENUE
    City, town or post office, state, and ZIP code   MONTCLAIR, NJ 07042

F   Accounting method: (1) ☒ Cash   (2) ☐ Accrual   (3) ☐ Other (specify) ▶ ....

G   Did you "materially participate" in the operation of this business during 2004? If "No," see page C-3 for limit on losses   ☒ Yes ☐ No

H   If you started or acquired this business during 2004, check here . . . . ▶ ☐

Part I   Outcome

1	Explanation, organization, motivation, decoration, instruction, introduction, definition, action, information, entertainment . . . . ▶ ☒	1	117,349.
2	Rejections and compromises	2	10,000.
3	Net Appreciation . . . . (subtract line 2 from line 1)	3	107,349.
4	Gross	4	
5	really Gross	5	
6	Add lines 5 and 6 . . . . ▶	6	107,349.

Part II   Process.

7	Procrastination	7	1,740.
8	Car and truck expenses (driving around a lot) . . .	8	890.
9	Interns, students	9	
10	Depletion	10	
11	Sleep deprivation	11	
12	Self-Deprecation (deduct total self worth from line 2) (use worksheet included in Part III) (see page C-4)	12	
13	Fringe	13	
14	Assurance (other than from spouse)	14	
15	Interests:		
a	Art, music, movies, books, radio etc.	15a	1,243.
b	Type	15b	757.
16	Plagiarism	16	
17	Office decorations	17	417.

18	Pension, profit-sharing plans (ha!)	18	
19	Upgrade from OS 9 to OSX:		
a	a perfectly good equipment thrown away.	19a	4,619.
b	b learning Indesign	19b	45.
20	Wait time on technical support phone calls	20	
21	Taxes and licenses	21	
22	Fraternizing:		
a	a Hobnobbing	22a	3,832.
b	b Consorting 756.	22b	
c	c Enter nondeductible amount included on line 23a (see page C-5) .		
d	d Subtract line 23c from line 23 .	23d	
23	Charrette	24	
24	Wages (less employment credits) .	25	
25	Other expenses (from line 48 on page 2)	26	

28	Deadline, due dates, drop-dead dates. . . . . ▶	27	
29	To file for an extension	28	
30	**For Paperwork Reduction Act Notice, see Form 1040 instructions.**	29	
31	Net profit or (loss). Subtract line 30 from line 29.		
	• If a profit, enter on Form 1040, line 12and also on Schedule SE, line 2 (statutory employees, see page C-6). Estates and trusts, enter on Form 1041, line 3.	30	90,030.

32a ☐ All design involves risk.
32b ☒ Some design involves risk

Cat. No. 11334P

Schedule C (Form 1040) 2004

Sustainability

Sustainability is clearly an issue of mounting importance to designers and the people they design for. Not only do designers create, or are at least complicit in creating, so much waste, but also their work is instrumental in helping the sustainability movement represent itself in ways that are more connected to the concerns of the contemporary consumer.

"I'm amazed at how slow graphic design is on the uptake with issues relating to sustainability," says Janine James, founder of multidisciplinary design firm The Moderns. "The other disciplines are much more advanced." Part of the reason for this is that graphic designers tend to be hardwired to place a high value on subtle visual nuance. The tote bag that James's firm made for a design conference is a case in point. The bag's fabric was made from a corn-derived polymer called PLA that can be either recycled or downcycled after use, and the bag's iconography referenced its own lifecycle. What caught conference attendees' attention, however, was the fact that the blue on the hangtag did not match the blue on the bag. This was because in order to match the silkscreen ink with the printer's ink, The Moderns would have had to use ink that contained heavy metals. "You wouldn't believe how many comments I got about those blues not matching," says James.

To James and her firm, good design is about communicating using materials that make the least possible impact on the environment. Troubling statistics show that printing inks and toners are the second-largest uses of carbon black, a substance manufactured primarily by the incomplete combustion of oil; and the pulp and paper industry is the third-largest consumer of fossil fuels worldwide, and one of the largest generators of air and water pollutants, waste products, and the gases that cause climate change.

Kristian Bodek is Research Scientist at the The Moderns. His job is to analyze all the materials that the firm specifies and review them for their environmental and human health profiles. He determines which print vendors to use by subjecting them to rigorous interviews. The warm-up questions include: "Do you recycle your print scrap, press rags, and processing chemicals?" and "Do you recycle your inks to make black ink?"

"When we're down to a couple of printers, we go a lot deeper," Bodek says. For example, he'll want to know if a printer goes direct to plate in prepress to cut out the chemical

process. Next, he'll investigate the inks that a printer uses. "Warm red is often created using barium. We ask: 'Is there any other way to get to that color without using barium?'" Bodek believes that, as a result of his actions and those of other like-minded design companies, printers are beginning to highlight in their marketing materials how environmentally responsible they are. All of The Moderns' research into materials feeds a deep database so that, as each project arises, they are able to determine which materials were grown, processed, transported, and disassembled in the least environmentally harmful way.

The materials misused in graphic design are not confined to the print world. E-waste, for example, is a troublesome byproduct of the industry. According to Tsia Carson, a partner at Flat, who has produced a digital viral Public Service Announcement on this issue, "People have this conception that electronic devices—things that have microprocessors—are very clean, when in fact the materials needed to make them are ecologically problematic. Plus, we generally don't dispose of them in a suitable way." Cyberspace seems much more substantial when you consider that 220 tons of computers are dumped in landfills and incinerators every year in the US.

Focusing good intentions on materials used and disposed of by the design industry—things such as paper, inks, plastics, and computers—is only one approach to sustainable design, however. An alternative

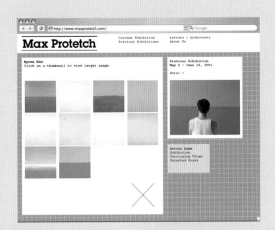

Left: AIGA conference tote bag
Made from a corn-derived polymer called PLA that can be either recycled or down-cycled after use. The bag's iconography references its own lifecycle.

Above: Max Protetch Web site
Designed by David Reinfurt. All text on the site can be easily edited and updated by gallery staff with no special programming skills necessary.

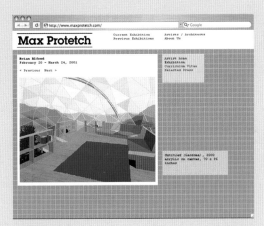

way to think about sustainability, aside from fixating on materials, is to think about it in terms of energy—both the designers' and the clients'.

Every piece of graphic design contains embodied energy—the time, passion, and talent that went into its making. "I'm amazed at how much redesign goes on," Michael Bierut, partner of Pentagram says. "People don't value graphic design because it's not thought to leave a hole when demolished." Bierut points to the tearing down of New York's original McKim, Mead, and White-designed Penn station in 1963 and its role in the subsequent emergence of the historic preservation movement in the US. "Whether it's the Paul Rand UPS logo or anything else, we have a pre-Penn Station mentality in the graphic design world. We tend to say, 'Let's knock it down and replace it with something else.' As long as we keep acting as if graphic design ideas are totally disposable, we'll have a lot of trouble developing a true culture of sustainability at any level in our profession."

Designing less and designing better is the primary goal of a new generation of designers interested in sustainability. Their aim is to create solutions so appropriate, so infinitely modular and forward-thinking, they reduce the client's need to keep having things redesigned. This puts greater emphasis on making systems that are open to change and can be easily updated—by anyone. This idea of "allowing things to be never quite complete" and relaxing one's hold on "really precise formal relationships" derives from the potential of electronic media and the need for Web sites to adapt and grow, says David Reinfurt, the principal of ORG. His

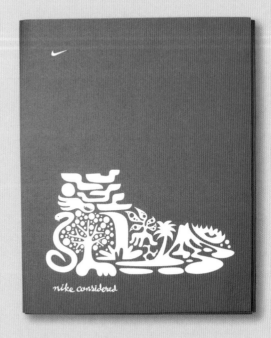

design for the Max Protetch Web site, for example, allows the gallery to update it monthly, every time it has a new show. Reinfurt has created a modular, scalable system in which information appears on the page in a series of boxes. The client can keep on adding the variously sized and colored boxes and, because they each have what Reinfurt calls "a discreteness," the pages continue to look coherent. Such a system allows for the site to grow exponentially.

Similarly, in Flat's interactive design work, they push database-driven solutions rather than Flashier experiences that can't be easily updated. "It may be less sexy, but it's something clients will be able to use for years," says Carson. This is the approach Flat used to inform their solution for Creative Time. The site, that can grow or contract as needed, is also a modular publishing system, enabling

the public art curatorial organization to produce direct from the site invitations, catalogs, and other publications.

Design plays a vital role in helping sustainability as a larger social movement to develop a more contemporary and resonant public image. Currently, it is not connecting with the public and is regarded as an alternative rather than an essential way of life. Its tone tends to be highpitched and pious, its visual references confined to woodcuts or wishy-washy illustrations of trees and leaves, and its color palette a limited range of browns and greens. "Unfortunately, these causes do themselves a disservice by sticking to the trees and leaves esthetic," says Mark Randall, director of design firm and non-profit organization World Studio Foundation. "We want something that's empowering and that speaks on an emotional level."

Considered packaging
Designed by Todd St. John for Nike's Considered collection that aims to eliminate waste and toxic substances during the manufacturing process.

Stephanie Smith, founder of Ecoshack, and a brand consultant in Los Angeles, recognizes this potential for design to permeate culture. She says, "Consumers need to get much more excited about sustainability. They need to be told that it's much more than a niche idea. Bringing more creativity to this stuff and more excitement and competition to the marketplace is key to triggering sustainability on a broader scale."

Change is beginning to happen within large brands. With American Apparel's new Sustainable Edition, made with 100 percent USDA Certified Organic Cotton, for example, is trying to brand around green issues and its edgy advertising has been successful at attracting a 15- to 25-year-old market. Hip jeans brand Rogan has a new line called Loomstate that also uses organic cotton and it's being talked about on youth and fashion blogs in reverential tones. Nike recently introduced its eco-friendly Considered collection that aims to eliminate waste and toxic substances during the manufacturing process. The branding is less splashy than Nike's other product launches; it relies on word-of-mouth recommendations and on an informative sitelet in which areas of flat color are built up in a Flash animation. It feels cool, contemporary, and understated, but without a twig or a leaf in sight.

Future Farmers, a design firm in San Francisco, is hot-wiring its green-infused interactive work by tapping into the visual currency of video games. There's *Seed Savers*, for example, an anti-GMO game, in which a player's goal is to help a character called Pinga capture pollen and redirect butterflies and moles from GMO plants, and more information about the topic can be found in a section titled "Subplot." Solar Generation, a decidedly funky action Web portal for Greenpeace is another project in which Future Farmers' founder Amy Franceschini is helping to chart a contemporary, culturally relevant graphic language for sustainability. The site, with its bright colors and video-game-derived iconography of solar panels and wind turbines, serves as a portal for an international community of alternative-energy activists.

Today there are growing numbers of designers who embrace the idea of design being something that changes, mutates— even decays—over time, and the loss of control on their part that this implies. A new generation of designers is experimenting not only with what culturally connected sustainable design could look like, but also with what it doesn't look like, because truly sustainable design allows for the contributions of multiple authors in unexpected ways over time—the kinds of change that haven't even been imagined yet.

Solar Generation Web site and *Seed Savers* game
Designed by Future Farmers. Solar Generation is a Web portal for Greenpeace, featuring bright colors and video-game-derived iconography of solar panels and wind turbines. *Seed Savers* is a video game whose main character, Pinga, captures pollen and redirects butterflies and moles away from GMO plants.

WHAT IS GRAPHIC DESIGN FOR?

Art Chantry, Seattle, US

"Before I say what I think graphic design is, I need to start by pointing out what it isn't. It isn't art. Graphic design may look like art: created through a process that appears the same as art; be treasured by some as art; or hung on the wall like art… But it's not art. That is like saying a dentist and a doctor are the same thing—we know that they are not.

"Graphic design is not a muse-driven statement by an individual in dialog with other artists, critics, museums, and curators. Graphic design is the collaboration between a designer and a client to create a piece of advertising or promotional material. What a graphic designer creates is a bit of marketing propaganda, a piece of folk art for a technological merchant culture, a functional statement promoting a product, a candidate, an event. Once that function ends—the product discontinued, the candidate forgotten, the event over—then what is it? It's not art, it's an old advertisement. I say it is a cultural artifact. Graphic designers don't produce art, they produce artifacts.

"An artifact is actually a piece of language and graphic design is probably the oldest language form known to mankind. Be honest—the written word is graphic design—little squiggles that, in combination, create larger concepts. The oldest cave paintings were not art, not muse-driven decorations, but functional, magic images. They were so functional, in fact, that once their function was used up, the magic hunt enacted, then they were disposed of like an old beer can. They were literally painted over with a new magic image to be used in the next magic hunt. Fine art cultures and disciplines grew out of the language of graphic design, not the other way around.

"Graphic design is language. It's a language of line and color, texture, shape, and form, etc. When we chose 'yellow', we are making a statement. When we chose a circle instead of a square, a ratty line instead of a clean line, we are saying something. Yellow means something to all of us. A square means something to all of us. Everybody understands what it means, but nobody realizes they know they understand what it means—except graphic designers. It is our language that we control and use to speak to the viewer. We use our language skills to change the mind of the viewer—buy this product, vote for this candidate, go to this event—and we do it for whoever is willing to pay us to do it. We are very powerful people in our culture, but we sell our powers indiscriminately, without regard for who is using our powers to what ends. If we are considered a service industry, then it begs the question: who do we serve?"

John Maeda, MIT Media Laboratory, Massachusetts, US

"For paying the bills"

Burkey Belser,
Greenfield/Belser Ltd, Washington DC, US

Luba Lukova, Luba Lukova
Studio, New York, US

"Pygmalion. Graphic design brings a thought to life, allowing you to engage the thought. At this point, it's tempting to write about the character of the 'thought,' the qualities of 'life,' and the nature of the 'engagement.' The exercise is certainly worthwhile but, stripped bare, this is what graphic design is for."

Nutrition Facts

Serving Size 1/2 cup (114g)
Servings Per Container 4

Amount Per Serving

Calories 260   Calories from Fat 120

	% Daily Value*
Total Fat 13g	**20%**
Saturated Fat 5g	**25%**
Cholesterol 30mg	**10%**
Sodium 660mg	**28%**
Total Carbohydrate 31g	**11%**
Dietary Fiber 0g	**0%**
Sugars 5g	
Protein 5g	

Vitamin A 4%	•	Vitamin C 2%
Calcium 15%	•	Iron 4%

Craft and complexity

There is a renewed interest in looking at the practice of design in close up, at the local level of making. At this local level, the textures and traces of the *craft* of graphic design begin to reveal themselves, and many designers, alienated by the slick finishes produced by a limited range of ubiquitous software applications, have discovered that the process of making things is both physically rewarding and a rich territory for investigating meaning.

Many designers are leaving their computer monitors to dust off outdated technologies such as the letterpress, to relish the feel of making things again. Judging by the amount of books, exhibitions, and conferences on letterpress, the handmade, handwriting and craft, and work bearing the mark of the hand, it's clear that craft—albeit a re-envisioned and contemporary take on craft—is a resonant theme amongst today's designers. Designer Lorraine Wild predicted many of these sentiments in 1998. In an article called "The Macrame of Resistance," published in *Emigre* magazine, she talked about the kind of knowledge that is developed through the skill of making something by hand. The idea of having an eye or an instinct is hard to rationalize, she says, but it is fundamental to design that expresses individual voice. Wild concludes her essay by saying, "The knowledge gained through activities that can be described as tactical, everyday, or, simply craft, is powerful and important, and it must form the foundation of a designer's education and work. Why else are we here?"

British designers Kristine Matthews and Sophie Thomas got hooked on using hands-on technologies such as letterpress and screen-printing while they were both studying at the Royal College of Art in the mid-1990s. Since forming their own practice in 1997, they have often sought recourse to this method of generating type, to avoid, "Sitting at a tiny desk staring at a screen all day, using only one finger to design everything." In a campaign to discourage the use of crack cocaine, the designers say they turned to letterpress because they, "Wanted a gritty feel—something that was rough and real and felt quite raw." The campaign's materials were printed using vegetable-based inks and recycled paper.

Part of the challenge of this job was coming up with a name for the campaign. The designers' proposals were bold titles such as Safe Streets and CrackOut. Such words lent themselves to the blocky treatment of letterpress, so the designers got permission to print up some mock-ups in the Royal College of Art's letterpress department one evening. In their presentation to Lambeth Council and the Metropolitan Police, they showed mock-ups of posters that featured big type in black and white. "I think the dramatic feel of it and non-slickness won over the committee," says Matthews.

thomas.matthews now has its own small letterpress set-up in their studio so that, as Matthews puts it, "We can stop bugging the RCA and Alan Kitching [a long-time promoter of the technique and one of its best-known practitioners] with requests." They've established a workshop space as part of their studio which has a huge screen-print bed, the letterpress, and, what the designers describe as, "Lots of odd equipment to play with—badge-making machines and such."

CRACK OUT

tackling crack cocaine in Lambeth

Crack Out campaign graphic
Designed by thomas.matthews.
The materials were designed
using letterpress and printed
on recycled paper using
vegetable-based inks.

Letterpress Scrabble
Designed by thomas.matthews.
Designers at the studio find
using wood type so satisfying,
they now have their own small
letterpress set-up.

"We Try Harder" painting by Hektor (right) and "Hektor Meets William Morris" (above)

For the "We Try Harder" piece, Jürg Lehni collaborated with the Swiss designer Cornel Windlin. In "Hektor Meets William Morris", Hektor was challenged to reproduce Compton, a wallpaper pattern designed by William Morris in 1896. This was the first design made by Morris specifically to be reproduced by a machine.

Using wood type, says Matthews, "Is entirely different from using a computer. The results are immediate for a start—what you see is what you get, no shunting it off to the printer with fingers crossed." Thomas and Matthews also enjoy the way in which the process generates mistakes and "happy accidents" that can be incorporated in the finished piece. "It keeps your design eye alert. You're really seeing things afresh as they come off the press (or get crumpled up accidentally and look amazing anyway)."

They also relish the technical skill involved in setting metal type, letter by letter. "It can be painstaking, but it gives you a huge appreciation for letterforms, letter spacing, and the real meaning of leading—they really are pieces of lead!" As for the limitations of letterpress, they say, "These can be liberating: do you *really* need to be able to set your type in every point size under the sun? Or stretch it 120 percent? If you do, maybe you better reevaluate your design solution."

Design's current reinvestigation of making is not limited to the technologies of yesteryear, however—code can be crafted, too. Hektor is a Graffiti Output Device that was built by Jürg Lehni and Uli Franke for Lehni's diploma project at the École Cantonale D'art de Lausanne (Écal). The contraption consists of a suitcase that contains two electric motors, a spray-can holder, toothed belts, cables, a strong battery, and a circuit board that is connected to a laptop and controls the machine. The motors that are mounted onto the wall suspend the can holder through the toothed belts and define its position by changing the length of these belts.

To create Hektor, Lehni first had to create "Scriptographer," a plugin for Adobe Illustrator that extends its functionality using Java scripting and translates vector drawings into paths that Hektor can trace with its spray can. "Scriptographer puts the tool back in the hand of the user," says Lehni.

For Tourettes II, a week-long program of performances organized by designers Stuart Bailey and Will Holder (Goodwill) in Amsterdam, 2004, Hektor was challenged to reproduce one of William Morris's wallpaper patterns on the wall of Gallery W139. For four evenings, Hektor steadily covered the wall, section by section, with Morris's 1896 design. The drips and runs became part of the piece itself—simultaneously precise and messy.

Lehni relishes the handmade quality of his digital tool: "It is kind of clumsy, like something made by two boys who spent their summer vacation tinkering in a basement."

The resurgence of interest in craft today, evident in product design, architecture, and fashion, as well as graphic design, is closely linked to a new attention to decoration, ornament, and pattern that manifests itself in the incorporation of handcrafted elements into manufactured products, and labor-intensive uses of technologies, both low and high. In the past few years, the pages we turn, the screens we summon, and the environments we visit are sprouting with decorative detail, geometric patterns, mandalas, fleurons, and the exploratory tendrils of lush flora. One of the impulses running through this work is a kind of stubborn celebration of uselessness. The modernist-derived philosophy that has dominated 20th-century design empties ornament of meaning and separates it from function, thus rendering it superfluous in the eyes of the canon. Knowing this, the feting of ornament and the production of exuberantly excessive, dense, and sometimes exaggeratedly useless work, therefore, can be seen as a provocative thumbing of the nose to the approach to design advocated by many schools and professional organizations in which "problems" are "solved" by following a sequence of codified steps. As Denise Gonzales Crisp, chair of graphic design at North Carolina State University puts it," The decorative speaks to the people using design and not just the clients who commission it. The super-rational approach to design seems to be all about the client—the idealized client."

Among this dense forest of fashionably ornamental graphic design is work that stands out because, in addition to irreverence and fun, it brings complexity, meaningfulness, and a seriousness of intent. Sometimes the decorative elements in a piece of work are not merely sampled from a palette of choices, but emanate directly from content and are integrated at a deep level with concept. They do as much work as the word in communicating. What does it take, then, to produce this kind of work? It may have to do with the extent to which a designer is involved and obsessed, even, with what they do. Involved and obsessed mentally, as Armin Vit points out in a discussion on Speak Up, stimulated by the subject of decoration, "Heavy ornamentation requires a type of character not found among many people. It's a balance of obsessive compulsiveness, an acute sense of style,

and an understanding of when to stop." But also involved and obsessed physically—with the making of the thing.

The relationship between craft, decoration, and ornament is a longstanding and a close one. The Arts and Crafts movement helped to reinvest handcraft with social value. William Morris was famously opposed to the mechanization of craft activity but, more recently, the design educator Malcolm McCullough has written about the idea of the computer as a craft tool. He extrapolates "digital craft" as, "A blend of skill and intellect accompanied by a blend of work and play, use and beauty, tacit and codified knowledge." The intricacy necessary to make patterns or construct ornament suggests more attention is paid to the craft of making and to detail. Gonzales Crisp also sees the computer as a key technology in the evolution of work that uses decoration in a meaningful way. "Amplification, complexity, and detail are key to decoration," she says. "And the computer lets you do that. You can noodle the heck out of anything now if you are inclined. It feels like this powerful tool that allows complexity that only craftspeople value. It reintroduces that connection to the making that maybe we lost with the über-designer handing off of stuff for production to a typesetter, lithographer, platemaker, and so on. It's like it's come full circle."

In product design, this connection between the decorative, detail, and craft is already acknowledged and is being probed. In this field, there is an emphatic and renewed interest in the humanness of making, and the "tacit knowledge" of making to which McCullough refers. Dutch design critic Louise Schouwenberg writes in depth on the subject. "Freed from its negative connotations, craftsmanship can be valued for the psychological effect it exerts on its user: it not only refers to a slower pace, but also implants this deceleration, and the implied attention to detail, into the product," she says.

Product designer Hella Jongerius, who has created an upholstery fabric for Maharam that has an unusually long repetitive pattern inspired by the jacquard cards (like early IBM computer mainframe punch cards) that tell the loom what to weave, and reconfigures in her ceramics and textiles archetypal patterns like *pied de poule* and bird and vine, talks of: "The power of decoration, which can transcend the visual to take on a different meaning." She embeds questions in her exaggeratedly ornate Swarovksi chandelier so that the decoration is put to work and asks critical questions. Jongerius was a founding member of Dutch design collective Droog that, in 1998, held an exhibition called "Inevitable Ornament." This idea of an inevitable connection between ornament,

MTV Sports and Music Festival titles
Designed by Todd St. John, HunterGatherer. These scenes were constructed using painted cardboard and the figures were animated by hand. The raw and handmade appeal of the animation is complemented by a soundtrack of the noises and laughter made by St. John and the designers at HunterGatherer as they participate in the making of the movie.

Collages for Ed Fella Web site
Designed by Ed Fella. Fella is a former commercial artist and a faculty member of the California Institute of the Arts whose hand-rendered letterforms found in his self-published works and numerous sketchbooks are highly individual reinvestigations of the craft of typography. These collages were constructed for use on Fella's Web site.

form, and content is something that graphic design is beginning to deal with right now. Gonzales Crisp has given this notion the label "decorational." By fusing concepts that tend to be seen as oppositional, she attempts: "To engage the discourse of ornament with that of rational design," and to suggest that, "Function is *completed* by ornament." The decoration we're seeing today is very particular to the time we live in. In many ways, it's dystopian. There's the inclusion of urban, dark, and ironic themes, as evident in Geoff McFetridges's attitude-laden takes on patterning in three designs titled Red Dawn, Stoner Forest, and All Yesterday's Parties. The latter design features camouflage patterns overlaid with a pattern of party detritus (beer cans, bottles, and cigarette butts). Similarly, Maureen Mooren and Daniel van der Velden's identity for the Holland Festival uses the argyle patterns that the typical middle-class Festival-goer tends to wear as windows onto apocalyptic images, and interweaves street trash with stained glass to create a tense critique of contemporary Dutch society. Even the voluptuous floral wall mural that extended the length of a block in the New York Prada store provided a frame for its own commentary. The installation was created in 1999 by design firm 2 x 4 in collaboration with Rem Koolhaas's Office for Metropolitan Architecture, and was among the first and most prominent of recent reinvestigations of pattern. It uses the silhouettes of full-bodied leaves and flowers as windows for photographic images that reference what designer Karen Hsu describes as: "Italianness, consumption, fashion, manufacturing, beauty, and sex."

"The rational aspect of the decorational is its capacity to tell, not only in a story-like way, but also in a metonymic way in the same way that icons do," says Gonzales Crisp. If there's a key or operative word to describe what's exciting about the best decorational work, says the designer, then it's "complexity." She explains: "Life is very complex and much of graphic design's time gets spent on refining and organizing and making things clear. There are all kinds of ways to think about graphic design's service, however. It can also be about establishing empathy or providing escape."

What will give decoration, pattern, and ornament life beyond that of their current popularity, then, is the fact that they provide designers with an alternative to orthodox views of design's role as a solver of problems and a simplifier of things. They are strategies for thinking and making that have rich histories but that can be continually reimagined. They can be used as framing devices or carriers for critical or narrative commentary. As Van der Velden says, "Playfulness and layers, multiple narratives, embedding history, seeking relations, and also political implications are better expressed in a visual vocabulary less dogmatic and more rich than modernism."

Milton Glaser, New York, US

"The purpose of graphic design is to move people to action or to inform them. If part of that role is to create a benign social environment, so much the better."

Andrew Sloat, Drainage Ditch, New York, US

"At my boarding school, the dress code for boys was rigid: a jacket and tie (or jacket and turtleneck), no jeans or other pants with pockets sewn on the outside, no sneakers. But, being prep school boys, we did our best to look as terrible as possible to show how good we were at flouting the rules. The rich kids wore nice clothes, but with too many clashing patterns; the hippies wore things big and old; the kids going through growth spurts wore strange sets of hand-me-downs. I wore the same thing every day: a turtleneck, a cheap houndstooth blazer, khakis, and Birkenstocks with wool socks. I'd slip off the blazer and sandals once I sat down in class. I looked like I was wearing pajamas.

"At the time, I could never understand why the school insisted on keeping us in dress code; surely we'd all look less ridiculous if we were allowed to choose our own clothes. But despite our persistent, bratty dissent, the administration remained firm, because while it may not have made us look like little businesswomen and -men, it made class time distinct. In a residential school, where everyone and everything was always the same, the six and a half hours when you looked different helped prioritize the most important part of the day. The dress code distinguished the classroom hours from the rest, made them more difficult to slouch through.

"Graphic design is marching our visual world back to its dorm room and telling it to put on a tie. Any tie."

Lucienne Roberts, sans+baum, London, UK

"What is graphic design for? Gosh, this is a taxing question. But it's a good one, because it implies that graphic design does something and can make a difference. It also leaves the door open for despairing answers like 'God only knows' and 'who cares'.

"Graphic design is the visual representation of a message that is not usually the graphic designer's. Most graphic design is commissioned by clients who have a need to communicate their message to someone else. That's actually what makes it important. We have a responsibility to choose which messages we wish to endorse, since our work will make it travel further and can change the way it is interpreted.

"Graphic design is a determining factor in how the message is received. It can make it more transparent, it can give emphasis or encourage different interpretations. It can amuse and entertain. It can make even the simplest of objects more pleasurable to use. It can make the world a more beautiful place and work better, too, and the wonderful thing is that it is fundamentally egalitarian—seen and used by everyone."

John Fulbrook, Simon & Schuster, New York, US

YOUR AD HERE

Graphic design is for people

Although most graphic designers agree that the people who receive and use their work are important, significantly fewer feel the need to research their audience or test their work prior to publishing it. Approaches to understanding design's audiences range from scientific analysis to mystical connections. "When I work," says Norwegian designer and musician Kim Hiorthøy, "I don't think about the audience. They are not on my mind at all. I only try to make it work for me." Hiorthøy explains: "I have a clipping from an interview with the Norwegian playwright Jon Fosse where he talks about a term [called] *stimmigkeit* which means, as I interpret it, 'in-tune-ness' or 'just-right-ness.' He says that when something reaches this point of having *stimmigkeit*, it contains an individual voice, and that, if something has this individual voice, it will be understandable by everyone.

"I suppose this is a way of saying we all have something that is the same, in us, and if that same-ness exists in your work it will speak to that same-ness in other people, I guess I, at least indirectly, lean on this idea a bit when I work. If it looks good to me, it will look good to other people, too."

Hiorthøy's series of CD covers for the label Smalltown Supersound use delicate fragments in painterly compositions that are evocative and ambiguous. Hiorthøy's work has found an audience both in the music and the design communities all across the world. And yet this idea of community is an uncomfortable one for the designer. "The idea that the recipients of what we do are all kind of a community makes it sound limited and group-ish in a way which I don't know that I hope it really is," he says. "Or, at least,

I don't really make things with those people in mind. On the contrary, I try very consciously not to. I actually find that I prefer a degree of isolation somehow."

Much of Hiorthøy's work is for small-scale cultural projects, of course, and such a poetic approach will not work for designers less remote from the prosaic concerns of the marketplace. Even in the commercial sector, however, there is still room for a variant of Hiorthøy's *stimmigkeit*. Vince Frost, for example, emphasizes the importance of intuition in the design process. "There's no amount of market research that can beat that," he says. "It comes from within you, your years of practice, what you feel is right, the clues that come from a project, a whole lineage of feelings and ideas. I use my intuition on every job I do because that's what makes me *feel* it's right. The client can be wrong." In the case of the Westfield shopping centers, which Frost was helping to rebrand, the clients wanted to market to a broad age range, and Frost felt it was better to talk to a smaller range of 22 to 32 year olds. Subsequent market research confirmed Frost's hunch. "A really important part of being a designer," Frost says, "is to be really open to external stimuli and to be sensitive, to listen."

"It's interesting how many of us see the choice between satisfying ourselves and satisfying the client," says Michael Bierut, partner of Pentagram, as part of a Speak Up debate. "Those people out there in the real world who actually get stuck with the end product don't seem to be getting much attention, the poor souls." Selecting a design direction often results in a struggle between

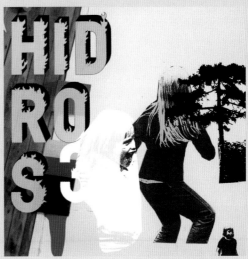

CD packaging
Designed by Kim Hiorthøy.
Hiorthøy makes beautiful and
enigmatic music packaging
for labels such as Rune
Grammofon and Smalltown
Supersound.

The CD covers shown here
are: Free Fall's *Amsterdam
Funk*; *Hidros 3* by Mats
Gustafsson/Sonic Youth
and friends; Lars Horntveth's
The Joker; and Jaga
Jazzist's *Magazine*.

Image

.

Maldoror

.

Text

Lautréamont 1846–1993
an international conference
at the Institute of Romance Studies
Cinema . Maldoror
at the Institute of Contemporary Arts
London May 26–30 1993

the designer and client over what would be best for an audience that is often poorly understood—it could be compared to two parents arguing about what is best for their teenager.

Ultimately, designers focus on the aspects of a project that they can control and seldom leave much room for audience involvement or alternate interpretations. The design press backs up this approach. Emphasis tends to be placed on the production of design rather than its consumption—on the designer as a creator of form and meaning, rather than on the reader as someone who can extract meaning but also add their own. Some designers do build in space for a user's input and experiences. Some designers do value the importance of research and take the time to find out about the people they are designing for. For most, however, information about the audience for a project comes to them via the filter of the client, if at all.

One form of feedback that comes directly from the audience is sales. When Frost redesigned *Creative*, an Australian magazine about creativity, the sales went up 50 percent and advertising up 30 percent.

"I'm always interested in how a book sells," says British designer John Morgan. "Especially when I've been involved in more editorial decisions, where I've helped the

final product take its form." Morgan shows more interest than most in what his audience might have to offer in the way of feedback. "I remember Jost Hochuli saying that when he designs a book, he always, 'Imagines the reader looking over his shoulder;' a sentiment I'm sympathetic with," he says. "Designers don't work in a vacuum." When Morgan, working with Derek Birdsall, designed the preliminary edition of the *Daily Prayer* book, they developed a questionnaire that was bound into the back of the 900-page book and that welcomed comments about content and layout from readers. This level of direct engagement with the reader or user, is a rare thing in graphic design.

The audience has received more attention from design academia, but primarily as an intellectual concern. Students and teachers associated with Cranbrook in the early 1990s were inspired by the writings of semiologists such as Roland Barthes, who in his 1968 essay "The Death Of The Author" said that, "A text's unity lies not in its origin but in its destination." They saw meaning as an inherently unstable entity and objectivity as an impossibility, and placed responsibility on the audience to interpret, decode, and read meaning in their work. In fact, in the opinion of Katherine McCoy, who ran Cranbrook's 2D program, graphic communication does not truly exist until each receiver decodes the message. In an article about deconstruction published in *Design Quarterly* in 1990, McCoy describes this kind of work as having: "An intellectual rigor that demands effort of the audience, but also rewards the audience with content and participation."

Image, Maldoror, Text poster
Designed by Paul Elliman for a conference on the work of the French writer Lautréamont. White boxes have been inserted between the words "Image," "Maldoror," and "Text", to allow conference participants to complete, alter, or negate the poster's message.

The Bubble Project
Designed by Ji Lee. Lee initiated "The Bubble Project" in 2001. He began a playful assault on image-based ads all over downtown Manhattan, placing blank speech bubble stickers on phone booths, city buses, billboards, and the New York City subway to provide people with a sanctioned space in which to write thoughts. Lee returned to photograph the responses and found statements of every kind, from political opinion to jokes, to articulate cultural commentary. Above all, he found the public interacting and communicating through the medium of graphic design.

For fields of practice such as game design, audience participation is a fundamental element in any design scenario. In graphic design, it is less common, but the idea of participatory design that challenges or invites the audience to take a role in the creative process has been revisited with some regularity. The idea of creating a framework that leaves elements to be completed by the viewer is especially appealing to those designers who prioritize systems and let predetermined processes determine form.

Daniel Eatock's utilitarian poster project has a skeletal framework and is dependent on audience participation. A generic form silk-screened on newsprint paper methodically guides the user through the steps of creating their own advertisement, and includes blanks to insert relevant information, such as titles of events, images, and people to contact.

A more recent example of the genre is Ji Lee's Bubble Project. Responding to the increasing amount of dull advertising he saw being used in public spaces, art director and designer Ji Lee initiated The Bubble Project in 2001. He began a playful assault on image-based ads all over downtown Manhattan by placing blank speech-bubble stickers on phone booths, city buses, billboards, and the New York City subway. Banking on the fact that people would recognize the graphic of the empty bubble as a place to write thoughts, Lee returned to photograph the responses. On the bubbles that hadn't been removed by authorities, Lee found statements of every kind, from political opinion to humor to articulate and profane cultural commentary. Above all, he found the

public interacting and communicating through the medium of graphic design. What began as an experimental interface in the public sphere has grown in recent years into a kind of movement with its own manifesto. Lee writes, "Once placed on ads, these stickers transform the corporate monolog into an open dialog. They encourage anyone to fill them in with any form of self-expression, free from censorship." The Bubble Project has mostly been localized in New York, but speech bubbles have started to manifest in other cities.

Focus groups and market research, which are popular among marketers and business people because they appear to provide an objective assessment of a product or promotion, are not popular among designers trying to find out more about an audience. As design educator Gunnar Swanson says, "All a focus group can really accomplish is to provide a check for designers' and or marketers' instincts: they reacted in a way we didn't expect? We should reexamine our thoughts either by changing them (and then testing more) or by reconfirming them. A focus group can help gather ideas. A focus group can let idea generators relax and say that they don't have important unanswered questions (or at least none that are worth trying to answer). A focus group can bring up issues that can be examined by other (specific or quantitative) research instruments. Anyone that tells you that a focus group is quantitative, scientific, or that it 'proves' anything should be fired on the spot."

And yet, the problem of how to learn more about the needs and reactions of graphic design's many audiences remains.

"The clients I have worked with in my short career are more concerned about what they like, rather than what will be appropriate for their audiences," says Ryan Nee, a young designer working in Denver on what he describes as "a lot of marketing campaigns." He continues, "If we expect to have any credibility, we need to remove a lot of the subjectivity out of our work by doing research—real in-depth research, not about what colors are hot this year, but about *people*. If we can sit across from clients and say, 'Look, we've really studied the people that you are trying to talk to, and we really think this solution works well because of these ten reasons,' a conversation will be started that will probably result in a good design solution."

The days when designers could rely on sharing a common cultural background and esthetic sensibility with their audience are behind us. As populations become increasingly diverse and customer needs more and more specific, designers who want their work to inform, delight, and connect, will need to know much more about the people they are talking to, their beliefs, and backgrounds. Designers will need to develop new strategies to navigate between their own culture and the heterogeneous audiences they serve. The importance of "real in-depth research" that Nee advocates, will only increase. This research needs to be integrated at the front end of design rather than as a token gesture in the guise of a focus group. "Human-centered design research encompasses a set of methodologies aimed at getting insight into what would serve or delight people," says

Brenda Laurel, Chair of the graduate Media Design Program at Art Center College of Design, Pasadena, California, and a champion of integrated design research. "It investigates behind the scenes, looking at individuals, situated contexts, cultures, forms, history, and even business models for clues that can inform design."

Such methodologies do not tend to be taught in design schools, let alone in graphic design programs. As design research does begin to assume a more central place amongst graphic design's concerns, and designers learn more about identifying, observing, and interpreting human behavior, it will be interesting to see how graphic design and the general public's understanding of it evolves. At the very least, as Nee suggests, "A conversation will be started that will probably result in a good design solution."

I am____ and ____posters
Designed by Rebecca Ross and Andrew Sloat for the LBGT Co-op at Yale University. This design allows each person to speak for him- or herself. The designers turned over the cliché "I am gay and proud" for reinterpretation by the university community. Students filled in the blanks on the 1,000 offset posters that were hung around campus in whatever way made the most sense to them.

ED FELLA:
What is graphic Reason for?

to make

SUGAR-FREE

CANDY

FOR THAT

eye

WHICH IS IN THE
ECONOMY
OF THE
beholder.

Jonathan Barnbrook,
Barnbrook Design, London, UK

"Graphic design is for meaningful exchange between humans, with the potential to tell millions something worthwhile which can change the course of society. Oh sorry, I meant it's the process with which corporations and advertisers shove messages that have no content, that we don't particularly want to know or care about, in our faces, at every possible opportunity."

Stefan Sagmeister,
Sagmeister Inc., New York, US

"Design is a language, so you can use it for complaining, entertaining, educating, agitating, organizing, money raising, mourning, denouncing, selling, and promoting."

Andy Altmann,
Why Not Associates, London, UK

"For wedging under the leg of a wobbly table."

Anatomy

Designers need to be fluent in many fields of specialized practice. Although they may still specialize in a particular medium, projects increasingly require the development of unifying concepts, broadcast through multiple channels. A rebranding project, for example, might involve the design of a new typeface and an interactive sound component as part of an identity program, the application. A designer may be expected to have expertise in such diverse areas as typography, animation, broadcast design, viral marketing, and game design. Creating an exhibition requires knowledge of working in 3D, the information-yielding possibilities of various interactive technologies, as well as the fundamentals of wayfinding signage and typography. This section represents a survey of several of these areas of practice. It focuses on those that are the most vibrant right now, due to their mutation, expansion, or collision with one another.

Most of the terms used to describe graphic design's various facets were codified around the middle of the last century, at a time when the discipline was becoming professionalized. Sixty years on, many of these descriptors—print design, corporate identity, logo design, etc—are inadequate to describe disciplines that are being shaped and reshaped by new economic and cultural imperatives. This means that many of the labels for design's component parts are in a state of constant flux and reevaluation. Since the emergence of interactive design in the mid-1990s, for example, this area of expertise has been variously known as Web design, digital design, experience design and, more recently, just design, as its boundaries have shifted, technologies have evolved, and its contexts expanded.

It might seem anachronistic to even try to dissect graphic design into parts like this. After all, in an era of multi-disciplinary practice, in which fluidity and flexibility are valued assets, what need is there to examine design within such a rigid, compartmentalized way? For the past decade, the focus of design has been on emphasizing the causal relationship between idea and form. Students now learn that a computer program can be picked up with relative ease and that what they should be focusing on instead is intellectual strategies, strong concepts, interesting stories, and considered approaches. From this perspective, the final form an idea takes—the medium through which it is expressed—becomes interchangeable and at times even irrelevant. At the same time, however, each medium has its own textures, peculiar qualities, and possibilities that, when understood and incorporated, can still enrich and inspire the whole. The way something is made is still vital to its meaning.

Experimental typography

Ever since the invention of printing, publishers, writers, printers, and designers have been experimenting with the ways in which type appears on the printed page. Eighteenth-century author Lawrence Sterne used typography to test how far he could push the novel's then-nascent form. In *The Life and Opinions of Tristram Shandy, Gentleman, 1759–67*, Sterne disrupts the flow of the text with blank, black, and marbled pages, as well as various typographic devices, such as asterisks and embedded images, to suggest to the reader such concepts as time passing, night, the continuation of dialog, and the meandering progress of his narrative. These playful experiments bring readers' attention to the visual character of the page, to the fact that the letter and the word are malleable visual forms that provide endless potential for creating and restructuring meaning.

In a similar plumbing of the semantic potential of page design, the French poet Stéphane Mallarmé produced a 20-page poem, "A Throw of the Dice Will Never Abolish Chance," that appeared in international literary magazine *Cosmopolis* in London, 1897. The traditional linear structure of text was replaced by a dynamic and open composition, combining horizontal and vertical movements and typefaces in different sizes. Like Sterne, the symbolist poet also made exaggerated use of white space to represent silence.

Another poet whose typographic expression comes closer to what we today recognize as graphic design is the futurist Fillippo Tommaso Marinetti. In pieces such as "A Letter from a Soldier to his Sweetheart in 1915," he tried to find the visual equivalents of sounds in the shapes and relative size of the words. Marinetti's program for a futurist literature anticipated many ways in which words came to be used as visual images in their own right in graphic design. "One must destroy syntax and scatter nouns at random... one should use infinitives... one must abolish the adjective... abolish the verb... one should deliberately confound the object with the image it evokes... abolish even punctuation."

Nearly all of the avant-garde movements of the early 20th century produced manifestos, posters, and other printed documents to promote their activities and codify their philosophies. The resulting expressive dialogs with the printed page have provided, and continue to provide, a vocabulary of typographic experimentation for designers to use and build on.

Allen Hori has designed many posters that are both beautiful and intellectually rigorous typographic explorations. Informational text is always well integrated in the body of the posters and Hori uses type as a vehicle to add his own meaning and interpretation of the event or concept that the poster is promoting.

Typographic experimentation is not confined to the 2D surface of the printed page, however. It finds 3D expression in the public realm when integrated into the facades of buildings, pavements, and plazas. In a piece such as A Flock of Words, a 984 foot (300 meter) long typographical sidewalk in Morecambe, UK, that leads visitors from railway station to seafront, and from Genesis to Spike Milligan in its trail of ornithological

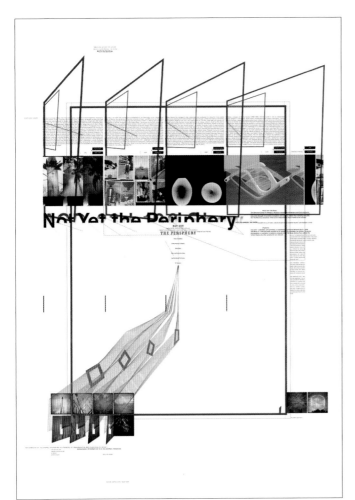

**Left: Not Yet the
Periphery poster**
Designed by Allen Hori for the
American Center of Design's
23rd annual 100 Show.
Typefaces used are Akzidenz
Grotesque, News Gothic,
and Rosewood.

**Below: Princeton University
School of Architecture
lecture series poster**
Designed by Allen Hori.

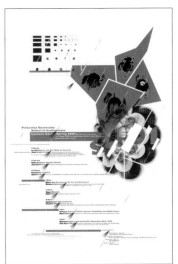

**Right: Spread from a book
about Beatrice Warde's
1955 essay "The Crystal
Goblet, or Printing Should
Be Invisible"**
Designed by Allen Hori.

Right: Argent type
Designed by Pierre di Sciullo,
seen here used in an exhibition
held in Chaumont, France.

**Below: Flock of Words
typographic sidewalk**
Designed by Gordon Young
and Why Not Associates. The
sidewalk is made from granite,
concrete, steel, brass, bronze,
and glass.

Left: Volvox fonts
Designed by Andrea Tinnes
with Martin Perlbach.

poetic and lyrical reference, Why Not Associates were forced to engage fully with the physicality of materials, and to think about the qualitative idiosyncrasies of interacting bodily rather than just mentally with typography. Letters set in Gill Sans and Perpetua are made from materials as various as granite, concrete, steel, brass, bronze, and glass. "Some of the materials come into their own when it rains," says Andy Altmann, partner at Why Not Associates. "A gray for example, turns to a deep black."

When working with type that people will walk on and around, the designers considered issues of public use and consumption of their work more fully than graphic designers normally do. Can a person walk forwards and read backwards at the same time? And, when wet, are certain materials too slippery to be safe? This work is a logical extension of the studio's mission to respond to what they perceive as people's willingness to engage with challenging and experimental graphic design. Among the precedents for such kinds of interaction with typography in the public realm is Maya Ying Lin's Vietnam War Memorial in Washington

DC, where visitors trace their fingers across the names of the war's victims carved into the polished marble.

Adding the fourth dimension of time enables designers to realize even more fully the dynamic potential of type that the early pioneers in this field first imagined. Many designers have animated type for music videos, commercials, and movie titles. Others, like Berlin-based designer Andrea Tinnes, conduct their typographic experiments using digital and interactive technology. Volvox is a system of five fonts that, through their superimposition, create a variety of ornamental composites. With the Volvox engine, the user is able to create an endless variety of colorful composites that pulse and rotate to the required specifications.

Uniting these disparate experiments is a stubborn refusal to accept a division between form and content. What a word says and the way that it says it are inseparable, and to neglect the letterform is to miss an important opportunity to enrich and transform meaning.

Movie titles

When the supremacy of the Hollywood studio system began to break down in the 1950s, newly independent American producers and directors, such as Otto Preminger and Alfred Hitchcock, were anxious to distinguish themselves both from one another and from the encroaching threat of television. One of the ways in which they branded themselves was through distinctive graphic identities.

Carmen Jones (1954) was one of the first movies to use this new method of visual differentiation. Its cohesive graphic identity was created by Saul Bass, one of the most important pioneers of movie title design.

Before this, movie credits consisted of titles painted on glass overlaid on artwork or appropriate backdrops. Pacific Title, founded in 1919, produced titles for *The Jazz Singer* (1927), *Gone with the Wind* (1939), and *Ben Hur* (1959). Pacific Title artists responded to the genre of the movie rather than its thematic preoccupation. Some of the visual clichés they engendered included rustic wood-grain type against a corral for a Western and script against lace or a rippling sheet of silk for a romance. In this context, Bass' work was revolutionary.

What Bass did was to identify a movie's most resonant metaphor and create a symbolic interpretation of it as the basis for the title sequence. From the mid-1950s until the mid-1960s Bass produced one graphically innovative sequence after the other. For *The Man with the Golden Arm* (1955), he chose an abstracted thrusting arm to evoke the film's exploration of heroin addiction; for *Bonjour Tristesse* (1958), an isolated teardrop; and for *Anatomy of a Murder* (1959,) a paper cutout of a corpse.

Bass' legacy lives on through the inspiration he provides for today's most successful title designers. Among them is Karin Fong, a partner of the Los Angeles firm Imaginary Forces. Her work, while various in scope, is consistent in its wit, emphasis on the physical craft of making, and its visceral graphic appeal. She has developed numerous award-winning sequences for blockbuster feature films, including *The Avengers* (1998), *The Truman Show* (1998), *Charlie's Angels* (2000), *The Haunted Mansion* (2003), *Dr. Seuss' The Cat in the Hat* (2003), and *Hellboy* (2004).

Among Fong's most recent projects is the sequence for the movie *The Prize Winner of Defiance, Ohio* (2005), which is based on the true story of Evelyn Ryan, a devoted housewife and mother of 10 in the 1950s. Her husband can't seem to make ends meet, so the enterprising Evelyn defies the conventions of the day and keeps her family financially afloat by entering and winning jingle-writing contests. To recreate an atmosphere of the world of contesting for the movie's title sequence, Fong and her design team used actual contest forms, prizes, images, and ads from the 1950s.

"It was important for us to remain true to the contest era," explains Fong. "Esthetically, we kept the titles inspiring and moving to celebrate this woman's resourcefulness and dedication to her family. Our goal was to bring the audience into this time period and world, and make them understand the nature of these jingle-writing sweepstakes."

The Prize Winner of Defiance, Ohio titles
A Dreamworks movie directed by Jane Anderson. The titles were designed and produced by Imaginary Forces, the creative director was Karin Fong, and the producer was Greg Talmage.

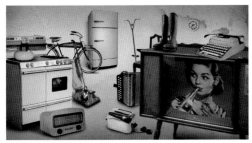

Visualizing music

As electronic music and DJs began to supersede the live rock band performance in the 1970s and 1980s, more visual stimulation was needed to keep audiences entertained. At the same time, video projectors and multimedia computers became increasingly accessible. A confluence of these factors in the 1990s led to the emergence of a new breed of visual practitioner—equal parts filmmaker, designer, and performer—the VJ.

The VJ's basic hardware consists of laptops, DVD players, video mixers, monitors, and live cameras. The software varies according to personal preference. Mumbleboy, aka Kinya Hanada, is a Japanese VJ currently living in New York. He uses programs such as Flash, After Effects, and QuickTime to make his whimsical animations, which he then mixes live. Sometimes he sets up a video camera above a big drawing pad. Then either he or audience members can draw on the paper and see it on the big screen being mixed in real time with preprepared images.

United Visual Artists (UVA) are best known for their collaborations with U2, Massive Attack, and Basement Jaxx. Due to the scale of the concerts they are providing visuals for, they can leave less to chance and improvisation than a VJ working in a club,

who can respond instantly to the mood of the music and the crowd. They must take a more controlled approach to their visuals.

On U2's "Vertigo Tour," UVA and show designer Willie Williams used a programmable L.E.D. curtain which sparkled behind the band like a huge digital waterfall, surmounted by four I-Mag video screens relaying close-ups of U2 across a single widescreen canvas. The curtain is made from tiny L.E.D. ball-shaped modules called MiSpheres that hang 64-to-a-string on 189 strings. When the spheres weren't in waterfall mode, images by artists Julian Opie and Catherine Owens played across them. As well as being visible from 360 degrees, the MiSphere strings could provide pictures and patterns without blocking anyone's view of what was happening on the stage.

What began as an underground art form that made use of ad-hoc technologies and a subversive attitude has now become a visible discipline with its own awards, conferences, and commercially produced software packages. As it evolves, the live mixing and projection of visuals is becoming a more viable possibility for other areas of design such as environmental graphics, exhibition design, and interactive media.

Above: U2 "Vertigo" tour
UVA produced, edited, and
programmed the graphics and
video for a new system of L.E.D.
drapes called Barco MiSpheres.

**Right: Basement Jaxx
"Kish Cash" tour**
UVA used their custom software
Dragonfly2 to display the
visuals on BARCO D7 L.E.D.s.

Left: Massive Attack
UVA worked with lighting
designer Vince Foster to
create the overall design
and implementation for this
lighting and stage set.

Broadcast design

With more choice of channels than ever before and the possibility to digitally record what you want to see and to fast forward through inconveniences such as commercials and channel identities, broadcast designers are facing new challenges in the field of channel branding.

Broadcast design is responding to these challenges in different ways. Some channels and networks, like BBC2 and MTV, have robust identities that they continue to build on by frequently commissioning new firms to create inventive show trailers and idents that viewers actually want to watch.

BBC2 has a solid reputation for showing memorable short films in between program junctions that promote the channel identity. Since it began in 1964, the figure "2" has almost always been prominently featured, manipulated at first by revolving, mechanical models and from 1979 onwards, by computer-aided technology. The "2" has remained the same shape since the early 1990s but has assumed various guises, such as a remote-controlled car and a rubber duck.

In the summer of 2005, BBC2 launched a suite of branding devices that played across TV, radio, and the Web to promote and identify its new comedy shows. Until that

point, the BBC2 character had always been seen in an enclosed studio environment, but a new campaign, including ident sequences written by Charlie Mawer, executive creative director at BBC Broadcast, turned it into a fluffy rod and hand puppet, created by the Oscar-winning special effects firm Neal Scanlon Studios. They took it out into the real world, where it interacted with a dog in a park, and with comedians from BBC2 shows.

Another way in which today's broadcast designers respond to new levels of viewer choice is to embrace and incorporate the idea of convergence between motion design for TV and for Flash-based Web sites. The quality of video in interactive environments has improved greatly.

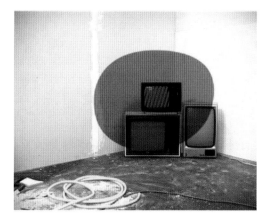

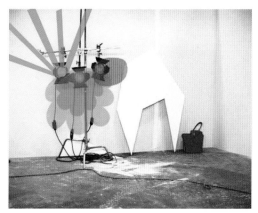

Above and left:
MTV UK idents
Designed by Sweden Graphics.

Right: BBC2 idents
Puppet designed by Neal
Scanlon Studios.

Sound design

The presence of sound—its qualities as well as its content—can convey complex information in powerful ways. Although sound has long been used in advertising and motion graphics, it is only in the past decade or so that graphic designers have begun to consider sound design as an essential component of projects such as wayfinding systems, exhibition design, and interactive design. One of the unique characteristics of sound as a design tool is that it has the ability to profoundly effect the way we experience other products of creative design. The advertising "jingle" recognizes the ability of sound to trigger an emotional response in the viewer. The "sonic signatures" that many companies use in advertising are now as recognizable as their logos.

As well as being used to convey information, sound can also transmit other layers of meaning, such as identity, emotion, and evidence of a specific place and time. Designer Ben Rubin incorporates sound into many of his projects, and pays particular attention to the ways in which sound can help people interpret data. "For years, I have thought about ways to hear inaudible phenomena, ways to map the observable world into the sound domain," writes Rubin. He collaborates regularly with architects, designers, and interactive designers. For a project called Listening Post (2003), he collaborated with statistician Mark Hansen to "listen" to activity on the Internet. "What do 100,000 people chatting on the Internet sound like?" the collaborators wondered. Instead of gathering data such as numbers of blogs, Web sites, stockmarket, or weather, they decided to use the language that pours

out of chat rooms every moment. Hansen wrote a software program able to extract information from chat rooms throughout the Internet and they constructed a grid of more than 200 small screens that display this text. An electronic voice reads the text, giving voice to tens of thousands of silent messages.

"Once Mark and I started listening, at first to statistical representations of Web sites, and then to actual language from chat rooms, a kind of music began to emerge. The messages started to form a giant cut-up poem, fragments of discourse juxtaposed to form a strange quilt of communication." The project was sponsored by Bell Laboratories and first shown at Brooklyn Academy of Music and then at the Whitney Museum in New York.

Subsequently Rubin was asked to propose a project for Adobe Systems' headquarters in San Jose, California. The project he came up with is called San Jose Semaphore (2003). The project consists of a series of eight illuminated discs mounted on top of the building. The discs turn to represent different coded pieces of information that spell out a text that Rubin has chosen. A synchronous sound track is broadcast on local AM radio so that anyone in sight of the building can pick it up in their house or car. The project not only generates sound through the radio signal, but also responds to sound in the environment. The building is right under the flight path of planes landing at San Jose airport, so when a plane flies over, the project picks up the noise and the disks spin as if suddenly blown by the wind. When the noise from the plane fades, they resume their steady transmission.

**Left: MIT Visual Arts
Center listening post**
Designed by Mark Hansen
and Ben Rubin. Photo
courtesy of the artists.

**Below: Whitney Museum
of American Art
listening post**
Photo by David Allison.

Games design

The design of video games has advanced dramatically in recent years. From *Halo* to *Half-Life*, *Grand Theft Auto* to *Jet Set Radio*, the design of game environments, characters, and player interfaces continues to evolve and, as it does so, to encroach on cinematic territory. With a new generation of more intuitive game consoles (where the gamer's own physical actions are used to input instructions), more subtle narratives being introduced, and more lifelike graphics being released, the line between the worlds of film and game development is blurring. One such convergence of the two genres can be found in the machinima phenomenon, in which low-budget films are made within a real-time, 3D virtual environment, often using 3D video game technologies. Another example is the *King Kong* game, created by Peter Jackson, director of the *Lord of the Rings* trilogy. Jackson wanted the video game screen to resemble a movie experience. On-screen bar graphics—usually used to show how much longer players have to live and what resources they own—have been replaced by a visual effect that turns the screen blood red if the player is dying and an airplane that flies overhead to airdrop ammunition. Such correspondences between the movie and the game experience do not necessarily lead to innovative design, however. Some say the success and concomitant constraints of the video game market are breeding a culture of safe design solutions.

Perhaps the most innovative work in game design is going on not inside the computer but beyond it—at street level—in the form of large-scale, multiplayer games that take place in the real world. A "big game"—as

their makers refer to them—might involve transforming an entire city into the world's largest board game, or hundreds of players scouring the streets looking for invisible treasure. *Superstar* is a game that took place in Tokyo for a month in 2005. The game used Japanese Puri Kura sticker clubs and the ubiquity of phone cameras as a starting point for a playful experiment in social networks. The goal of the game was to get points by photographing the stickers of other players and by having other players shoot your own. Players had themselves photographed and the photographs output as a sheet of Puri Kura stickers. They registered for the game by shooting a picture of their sticker using a photocam, and sending it to the game's Web site. They then moved around Tokyo adding stickers where they went.

area/code founders Frank Lantz and Kevin Slavin are especially interested in the social dynamics of play and what they call: "The playful use of public space." They observe that, "Instead of the simulated worlds of computer games, big games transform the physical space around us into a shared game world, brought to life by the choices, actions, and experiences of the players." An earlier game, developed by Slavin was *Conqwest*, a citywide treasure hunt played by high school kids using cellphones in several cities in the American north west.

Consumer brands and advertising agencies are already using big games as part of multi-level campaigns. As Lantz and Slavin suggest, "Big games point toward a future in which socially aware networks, smart objects, location sensing, and mobile computing open up new ways for people to play."

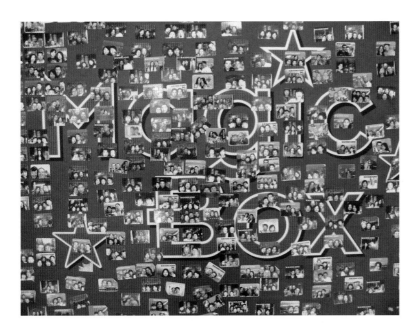

Superstar
Designed by Frank Lantz and Kevin Slavin of area/code, built by Komida, powered by Mobot mobile visual technology.

Signage

Urban spaces are used by different groups of people for different activities that take place at different speeds. Natives tend to be in a rush and just need to get wherever they're going—to get to a business meeting, visit a friend, pick up a package, catch a train, meet someone at the airport. At these times, you want a public space to be going your way, too, to unfold itself before you like a map, and to lead you deftly and with the minimum of fuss to your destination. In fact, you don't even really want to be aware that a wayfinding process is happening at all; all you want to think about is what will happen when you get there. Other groups of people, such as tourists, may have more time on their hands to take the winding route to their destinations. In some cases, the route itself may be the destination—especially if the city in question is a famously labyrinthine one like Venice.

Paul Elliman considered just such a conundrum when he and a team of students from the Werkplaats Typografie, Arnhem, were asked to propose a new signage system for Venice. "The inherent value of 'being lost' in a city is, ironically, what you might end up 'finding,' and a purely graphic approach to such a signage project would miss this quirk," says Elliman. "A conventional route to solving the problem of signage is, invariably, to produce more signage: a fact that befalls any area where the needs of tourism impinge on and sit alongside purely directional or geographical information (road signs, etc.)." Elliman and his team decided, therefore, to assist visitors by means of an audio guide, narrated by a fictional character called Salvatore, and accessible via cellphones and listening booths throughout the city.

In other environments, too, such as a museum, it's just as important to create a sense of atmosphere and institutional identity, as it is to provide unequivocal directional signage. When the Children's Museum of Pittsburgh expanded in 2004, Paula Scher and her team at Pentagram were commissioned to create the signage. Their solution emphasizes the character and attitude that environmental graphics can bring to a location. The new expansion by Koning Eizenberg Architecture bridged two buildings with a three-story structure that provides a new entrance and additional exhibit space. The architects crowned their expansion with a polycarbonate screen that links the buildings visually and, in collaboration with the environmental artist Ned Kahn, doubles as a shimmering wind sculpture made of thousands of plastic tiles that move in the breeze.

The signage program takes its cues from the expansion architecture. The letters of the marquee signage on the museum entrance extrude from the building and are lit by neon from within a wire mesh, creating dimensional letterforms that look like something out of superhero comics. Lobby signage and the donor wall are composed of colorful, fluorescent, Plexiglas panels. The color scheme is inspired by the lighting and by the museum's terrazzo flooring.

In the galleries, identification signage is composed of the playful treatments of words. Both scale and materials are exploited for humorous effect: "Garage" has been set in rubber tread; "Theater" appears forwards on one side of the doors and in reverse on the others, as though projected; and

"Studio" was created by kids painting through a stencil on the floor. The Nursery, a hands-on section for infants and toddlers, is wallpapered with pop graphics of giant baby heads. Throughout, the signage is inspired by the various activities of the museum and employs inexpensive materials and fixtures that are easily repaired or replaced. The signage typography is set in Futura and became so recognizably part of the museum's character, that the in-house graphics department has begun using the font as a de facto institutional identity.

Children's Museum of Pittsburgh signage and environmental graphics
Designed by Paula Scher, Pentagram. Photo by Peter Mauss/Esto.

Editorial design

New York Magazine, cofounded in 1968 by Milton Glaser, has a notable design heritage. In 2004, the magazine underwent a massive overhaul with the instatement of a new editor, Adam Moss, and a commitment from owner and patron Bruce Wasserstein of enough financial support to really make a difference. For the crucial position of design director, Moss hired Luke Hayman, a British designer living in New York, who was already well known both in publishing and design circles for his inspired art direction for design-sympathetic publications such as *ID*, *Brill's Content*, *Architecture,* and *Guggenheim*, but also for mass-market titles such as *Travel + Leisure* magazine, which received 14 Society of Publication Designers awards during his tenure.

Despite Hayman's natural leanings toward modernist design with sparse layouts and sans serif type, both he and Moss agreed that the redesign should reinvestigate and build on the magazine's design legacy, which was based heavily on classical typefaces and busy page composition. "We literally did go through the archives and pulled out and Xeroxed 'The Intelligencer' pages, and got a feel of what they were like in the 1970s and 1980s. Milton Glaser and Walter Bernard started it all. It was very smart and had humor, and the issue of illustration was very innovative. And then the Bob Newman/Kurt Andersen version had just such strength to it—Robert Best just did amazing things with type on a weekly basis before he had a computer. It just blows your mind when you see the amount of work he did."

From these seeds, Hayman and Chris Dixon, the art director, began to evolve a graphic language that referenced what Hayman calls the "bookish, classical typography" that was the magazine's visual legacy. They worked with a typeface called Miller which, says Hayman, "Comes in lots of weights and has a very elegant italic and small caps, and just lends itself to very elegant, classical, bookishness."

Part of the design challenge was how to create enough room for the numerous ideas the new editorial team wanted to include, in addition to the large amounts of service-based material that a city magazine features. Hayman recalls how Moss "told me what no editor has ever told me; he said, 'Make the type smaller, we have to fit more on here.'" They wanted it to feel rich with content but, says Hayman, "we didn't want to have everything screaming at you. And Adam was very much an advocate for elegance."

It definitely helps to have a design-sensitive editor to work with on a magazine, but true collaborative flow goes in more than one direction. The design team at *New York Magazine* is expected to attend and contribute to editorial ideas meetings. "We get our turn around the table to present ideas, and they often ask for visual ones, or photo-based ones," says Hayman. This kind of infrastructure—that allows for design and editorial to function on an equal footing—is what leads to real innovation and high standards in editorial design.

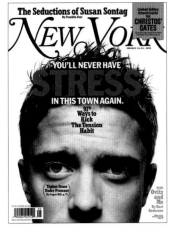

New York Magazine covers and spreads
Design direction by Luke Hayman and art direction by Chris Dixon.

Book design

The demands made of the contemporary book designer may seem conflicting and impossible to resolve: How can you design a covetable artifact that still works as a functional tool? How do you preserve the integrity of content while allowing your voice to be heard? How can you satisfy the demands of your various audiences—the publisher, the author, the marketers, bookstores, and the actual readers? Is there any room in such a complex and market-driven infrastructure for design innovation?

Traditional approaches to book design emphasize its physical form—a volume of many sheets bound together, containing text and images, with a spine for shelf identification, preceded by a copyright page—and believe that a book designer's role is to faithfully communicate an author's message to the reader, using the specialized and recognizable conventions of book design. Mary Mendell, a university press designer, has argued that, "What good book design is about is trying to set up an architecture for the book that is typographically sound and that helps the reader find the information he wants. It's not about putting the designer's personality into it."

And yet, as the American author John Updike says, an artistic creation such as a book is about a collaboration with the reader: "A book is an object, a work of manufacture whose many elements, from type and binding to quality of paper, are susceptible to esthetic criticism... but whose meaning has always had to be constructed, as a writer and a reader collaborate in imagining a series of scenes and events." Admittedly, Updike is referring more to fiction than to academic textbooks, but the idea that a book design, at its best, is a dialog both with the author's text and the reader's many possible interpretations, is a powerful one that applies across all publishing genres.

Many designers believe that a book is defined more by its purpose than its form and that, one of the roles of a book designer is to add their own critical take on the content—to shape, edit, or curate the author's material, to enhance the reading experience.

Perhaps this is because, faced with the threat of redundancy in a culture increasingly skewed to the digital, book designers are reinventing and repositioning themselves in an effort to validate their practice. And it's not just about the bold gestures—the haunting or humorous power of the book jacket, or the seductive visual narrative that draws a reader through a tome—it's also about the details. The positioning of footnotes or page numbers, the treatment of copyright information, chronologies, bibliographies, and indices—all these elements of a book, when treated with both dignity and imagination can lift a book from a utilitarian tool into a treasured and enduring object.

AIGA Year in Design 25
Designed by Barbara deWilde.

PERIENCE DESIGN | PACKAGING   BRAND + IDENTITY SYSTEMS DESIGN   TYPOGRAPH

{ 365 }

INDESIG

PERIENCE DESIGN   PACKAGING   BRAND + IDENTITY SYSTEMS DESIGN   TYPOGRAPH

{ 365 }

INDESIG

PERIENCE DESIGN   PACKAGING   BRAND + IDENTITY SYSTEMS DESIGN   TYPOGRAPH

{ 365 }

INDESIG

PERIENCE DESIGN   PACKAGING   BRAND + IDENTITY SYSTEMS DESIGN   TYPOGRAPH

{ 365 }

INDESIG

PERIENCE DESIGN   PACKAGING   BRAND + IDENTITY SYSTEMS DESIGN   TYPOGRAPH

{ 365 }

Information design

The main principle of information design is that it should make a body of complex data comprehensible and immediately accessible to its audiences. Traditionally, designers' engagement with this challenge centers on organizing data sets into well-designed charts, graphs, or diagrams of the type one finds in annual reports, in scientific text books, on food packaging… in fact, in every aspect of our day-to-day lives. When it's well done, the structures of information design recede quietly into the background and the information itself shines through. When it's poorly done, the consequences can be disastrous.

Increasingly, designers are departing from the printed page to explore other methods of data visualization that involve 3D and 4D, interactivity, and innovative uses of sound. For digital information, they are trying to liberate the user from the experience of sitting in front of a screen by integrating it into the architecture and the fabric of everyday life.

Information design is rarely, if ever, completely objective; most of it contains the designer's take on the subject matter being presented. In some cases—such as those with ubiquitous public value, like the Nutrition Facts label—it can be claimed that neutral information is being presented neutrally. The ingredients listed, however, are selective (a dairy product for example is not required to list the amount of hormones that the milk contains). When Burkey Belser designed the label in the late 1990s, it was revolutionary in providing consumers with information about what they were purchasing. Now, people want to know more. Not just about what a product is made from, but about where and how it was made.

Under the tutelage of engineer and artist Natalie Jeremijenko, students at Yale University have devised a Web application called HowStuffisMade (HSIM) that accumulates information about the way a particular product is made. The group wants to make their product profiles visible at the point of purchase and they are currently in negotiation to have them included as part of the product search engine, Froogle.

To date information design has been too much in service of business. There are other yardsticks, apart from the corporate one, against which to measure effective design. Obesity and changing demographics are just some of the forces reshaping the social landscape. Applying these new gauges can be as simple as rephrasing a question. For instance: instead of making a brochure to promote the airline with newly widened seats, in what ways can the designer have an impact both on the types of food served on that airline and the kinds of information about it conveyed at the point of choice? Or, for the growing multicultural populations, and disproportionately aging communities, what kinds of visual language systems can be employed to enable the easier completion of an application form? And, instead of more signage with bigger type in different languages, could the integration of something like sound design better facilitate navigation in the urban environment? These are just some of the questions that will define a new approach to information design for the 21st century.

Right: "Under the Weather" map

Designed by mgmt for *Harper's* magazine. The brief was to graphically show the linked relationship between increased rainfall, global warming, and the spread of infectious diseases such as cholera. The main challenge was to depict the different layers of information in a complementary but distinct manner, showing each layer independently but making the correlation evident. Numerical information on the cholera data ranged from less than 10 cases per country to nearly 50,000, requiring an icon system that encompassed the vast margin through scale and color. Information had to be easy to read as well as graphically appealing.

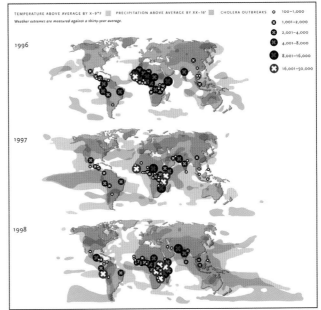

UNDER THE WEATHER

L ike many potentially fatal diseases ravaging the globe, cholera is both ancient and preventable. It is also on the rise, due in part to the varied effects of global warming. Between 1997 and 1998, the number of reported cholera cases worldwide doubled to almost 300,000, and deaths jumped by two thirds, exceeding 10,000. Cholera bacilli occur naturally in warm aquatic environments and flourish in excessive heat, their spread aided by heavy rains, both conditions pictured below. The drought and flooding associated with global warming increase the likelihood of transmission through tainted drinking water and food. Related disasters such as high winds and landslides hamper prevention and treatment, as do the highly concentrated or mobile populations associated with extreme poverty. Properly treated, fewer than 1 percent of cholera patients die; in recent years many countries have reported death rates eight times as high, eluding the medical advances—if not the greenhouse gases—produced by the industrialized world.

Map: Alicia Yin Cheng-, based on weather maps from the Climate Prediction Center and the International Research Institute for Climate Prediction, and on data provided by the World Health Organization. Research: Sara Lorimer; Paul R. Epstein, M.D., Harvard Medical School

Right: "14 Days in Iraq"

Designed by mgmt for the *New York Times*.

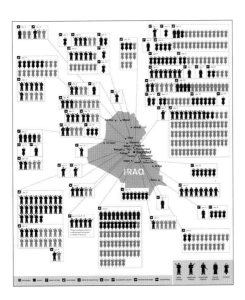

Interactive design

When Jet Blue Airlines wanted to move passengers through the check-in process more efficiently, it called on interactive design studio Antenna to help find a solution. Antenna studied the way that passengers move through the check-in process and then created an interface that helps customers select or change seats, check luggage, and print out their boarding pass. The kiosk manages to be friendly, approachable, and efficient. It gets customers to the gate quickly, and helps to communicate the "no frills" attitude of the airline. The design has helped to significantly increase the number of passengers the airline can accommodate and has helped to set Jet Blue apart from the competition.

But interactive design isn't always about getting someone through an experience quickly. Sometimes, it is about allowing people to slow down and take the time to enjoy a narrative or interpretative experience. When Urbis, a museum about contemporary urban life, opened in Manchester, UK, audiovisual specialists Land Design Studio created an interactive installation called "Imagining The City." The piece invites visitors to explore a range of creative responses to the concept of the city. Images stream across the horizontal surface of the installation and, with a sweep of the hand, visitors can select one of 128 items from menus labeled "City of Emotions," "City of Pleasures," "City of Imaginings," and "City of Senses." Digital fractals drawn from the item's source image are transferred onto an overhead panoramic screen, where a fantastic future city is built in real time by the combined activity of the community of museumgoers.

Another example of an interactive experience designed to engage participants in a more meaningful relationship with their environment is a piece called PowerFlower, created by Antenna. As people walked past the window of Bloomingdales on Manhattan's Lexington Avenue in the winter of 2002, motion sensors would trigger a row of 32 5-foot-tall (1.5 meter) neon flowers to bloom with light and sound. As soon as people noticed the effect their presence was having, they would wheel right around to the beginning of the window and walk its length again. Others noticed, some joined in, and some just stood and watched as passersby left a trail of lighted flowers and a pretty melody in their wake. Apart from its magical qualities (all the technologies were carefully hidden behind a seamless backdrop), the success of the piece lay in the fact that the flowers' responses to one's movements were so immediate and therefore comprehensible.

Interactive designers are focusing increasingly on the systems and applications that underlie Web sites and media installations, as well as on the interfaces themselves. This emphasis on systems is the result of the fact that designers are increasingly asked to create a design that addresses not only what something is, but also what it will become. A Web site, for example, may start out with 50 pages and grow to 5,000. The American Institute of Graphic Arts (AIGA) Design Archives, designed by the interactive design firm Second Story, displays over a thousand winning entries from AIGA's design competitions. Not only are visitors to the site able to view and cross-reference the entries in order to find all the entries from a certain

Above and left: Jet Blue Airways hardware and screen interface
Designed by Antenna Design.

Left: Cherry Blossom interactive installation
Designed by Antenna Design. Cherry Blossom was on display during the Design Triennial at the Cooper-Hewitt National Design Museum in New York, 2003.

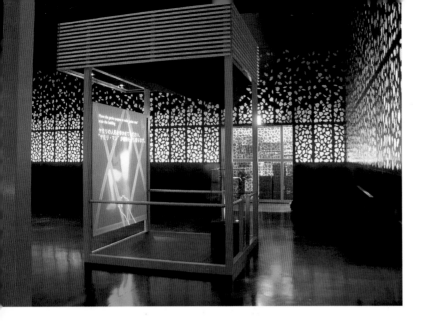

Left and below: Expo 2005
Designed by Land Design Studio. Land used single hand and sensory interfaces through which hand movements could make a shark swim and the air from a fan could open the scales of a digital pine cone.

year, in a particular category, or by a specific designer, they can also create collections of their own favorite winners, describe why they like a design, and share their collections with others. Each visitor to the site can, in effect, create their own miniature design museum. And each year the number of entries grows as new winners are added.

Most Web sites of any scale are managed by more than one person and need to accommodate change. Today's designers are being asked to devise strong but flexible systems that can contain, process, and present information in ways that are easy to maintain and easy to understand. Even if they are not actually building the applications that create this infrastructure, the designer needs to know how these systems function in order to understand the opportunities and limitations of the project.

Designers increasingly find themselves to be part of a system. As projects become far too large and complex for one person to handle, designers are required to collaborate with large teams, representing many skills.

Converting complexity into simplicity— creating simple interfaces at both the front and back end of complex sites—is one aspect of contemporary interactive design. Another approach that some designers, like Joshua Davis, favor is to move from simplicity toward complexity. They are building software that combines simple forms to make complicated patterns or that make complicated forms even more complicated. Davis created one such system to create a digital forest. He defined seven possible tree trunks and six different types of leaves. He also designed 15 things that could live in a forest. The software combined these elements using rules or algorithms to make what appears to be a living forest. Because the particular placement of the elements is random, the forest looks different each time the program is run.

Davis is now taking his work to the next level by creating systems that will not only make images but also learn which ones are beautiful—or at least beautiful to Davis. He calls this new kind of design the "Genetic Esthetic." Davis rates elements of the computer-generated compositions on a scale of one to eight and, over time, the computer learns what elements and combinations Davis finds pleasing and produces them.

Identity design

Until fairly recently, designing an identity for a corporation or an institution was about distilling the essence of that corporation or institution down into a single graphic mark or logo. This logo would then be applied to the various surfaces of a company's physical presence in the world—from letterhead to trucks—following the guidelines set out in a style manual. Now, however, as the contexts and uses of branding become increasingly complex, identities have needed to evolve into more flexible, multifaceted, and fluid systems that perform different functions for the different groups of people who encounter them.

With the opening in the spring of 2005 of the Walker Art Center's new expansion, designed by the Swiss architects Herzog & de Meuron, there was an opportunity for Minneapolis's premier forum for the arts to reinvent itself. "It makes sense to develop a new identity system to help signal a new institution," says Andrew Blauvelt, design director at the Walker. "The main question was: how can the Walker approach the idea of a graphic identity in a fresh way?"

Blauvelt says he wanted the new identity to be: "Visually distinct, conceptually and technologically unique, yet totally in the hands of the designer. It needed to have some very simple rules about application and work at a variety of scales: Small enough for a business card, but large enough for a wall." He also wanted it to build on, rather than replace, the Walker typeface designed by Matthew Carter for the museum in 1995. "Just as the architecture of our expansion does not ignore what already exists, a new identity must acknowledge what has come

before," says Blauvelt. The new identity incorporates the Walker font for specific purposes such as gallery titling and on a light box building sign. "The fact that we have an in-house staff responsible for the look and feel of all communications means that we exercise control over the design and can avoid the legacy of the style manuals and guides that render an identity static and eventually stale," says Blauvelt.

The idea for the identity grew as Blauvelt was thinking about the work of Daniel Buren, an artist who has used vertical striping as what Blauvelt describes as, "A kind of surrogate for the art object." Blauvelt began to think about a line—the simplest dynamic of geometry—and whether it could be used to represent the Walker. "Could it be as simple as a piece of tape?" he wondered. The designers knew that the identity had to fulfill many diverse functions. Sometimes, it would need to behave quietly within the context of other things; sometimes it would be alone and would have to perform in a more explicit and dramatic way. Blauvelt was interested in exploring whether the system

Top right: Instructions for using Walker Expanded
The Walker Art Center's identity functions as a typeface, but instead of using bold and italic fonts it is grouped into related words, or vocabularies, and repeating patterns.

Bottom right: Parking garage wall graphics
These demonstrate how the new identity can be applied to surfaces like a roll of tape.

Step 1   Select a font and choose a word by typing the corresponding character

 **WALKER ART CENTER**

Step 2   Delete space bar to overlap elements

Step 3   Choose a pattern

Step 4   Overlap the two lines by setting the leading to zero

Step 5   Repeat to create a line and customize the color

Above left: Notebook from
the Walker Shop

Above right: Walker
Shop bag

Left: Self-mailer envelope

could grow and change over time and whether there was, "A specific gesture that could be recognizable even if some of the elements were variable (like words, colors, textures)."

The identity they developed, known as Walker Expanded, sets lines of words, patterns, and textures that, like a roll of tape, can be applied to virtually anything—from printed matter and Web sites to merchandise and architecture. The identity is always recognizable as a line, but the elements that compose the line are variable.

Type designer Eric Olson worked with the team to develop the unique type-based system that generates the identity. It functions as a typeface but, instead of being organized into weights and styles like bold and italic, the fonts are structured around groups of related words. They operate like vocabularies, and can be tailored to specific audiences and specific contexts. One font, called Peer to Peer, is for use within the institution, while Public Address talks in terms more accessible to the general public. The shop has its own vocabulary-based font, too.

Chad Koepfler, a senior designer at the Walker, explains how it is used: "Once you have your word group chosen, you simply hit a single key to generate an entire word. For example, the 'D' key produces the word 'design.' The 'E' key gives you 'exhibitions,' all in the proper size and typeface. Also built into the font are different patterns that can be typed out and set behind a row of words."

Koepfler remarks on how the identity morphs depending on its purpose: "The program or subject and the audience dictates which word groups to use and how dynamically the identity appears." There is also the possibility that some of the vocabularies, such as the group of adjectives used to describe the Walker and its programs, will grow and change over time. Blauvelt foresees them being able to take and incorporate data from visitor surveys, for example. "In this way, this new identity becomes its own little record of institutional change over time," he says.

Advertising

In the world of advertising, creative capital is by no means dependent on size. Growing up alongside the massive global advertising agencies are increasing numbers of smaller boutique firms that have just as much impact on the brand landscape as the time-tested heavyweights. These younger, streamlined firms distinguish themselves through various approaches, such as the savvy use of irreverent humor and the fluid exploitation of multiple channels, including the viral potential of the Web. And among the most interesting of these agencies are those that locate design firmly at the center of their core philosophies.

Considering the deadpan and uncompromising sensibility of KesselsKramer, the Dutch communication agency founded in 1996, it should come as no surprise that their Web site is a rotating series of fake, badly designed Web pages for KesselsKramer Dating Club, KesselsKramer Swimming Pool Repair, KesselsKramer Pizza delivery, all replete with pulsating icons, gaudy banner ads, and textured backgrounds. It also makes complete sense that when you open the door to their office on a side street in Amsterdam, you find yourself in a church.

Their long-running campaign for the Hans Brinker Budget Hotel in Amsterdam—in which all the drawbacks of a bad youth hostel are highlighted as desirable features: dogshit on the doorstep, no toilet roll, stained pillows, one bathtub for 354 rooms, severe bruising after a night's stay—is typical of KesselsKramer's approach. Their work speaks in a no-nonsense, direct-verging-on-rude, no-make-up, real-sound-in-the background kind of way. In addition to the

Hans Brinker, KesselsKramer's other local clients include the Amsterdam newspaper *Het Parool*, a coffee shop close to the studio, and a hairdresser. At the other end of the spectrum, there's Nike, Audi, and Diesel. KesselsKramer's interests and activities extend well beyond advertising to making documentary films—one was of a match between the two lowest-ranking soccer teams during the 2002 World Cup—music videos, publishing books, and organizing exhibitions. Perhaps that's because, as the firm's cofounder Erik Kessels has said, "It's good to know where one discipline starts, but it's always better to ignore where it ends."

not included

I am**sterdam**.

**Above: Hans Brinker
Budget Hotel poster**
Designed by KesselsKramer.
The designers use reverse
psychology to promote this
low-budget backpackers
hotel in Amsterdam.

Left: I Amsterdam campaign
Designed by KesselsKramer.
The motto "I Amsterdam" was
devised by KesselsKramer in
2004 as part of a larger
campaign to present a more
robust profile of Amsterdam
to internationally active
enterprises, business visitors,
and tourists.

Type design

While the number of designers who specialize in designing and distributing typefaces remains relatively small, those that try their hand at designing one or two, is clearly on the increase. Programs such as Fontographer have opened up the possibilities for font creation, and using Web sites as storefronts has facilitated distribution, making type design a more appealing and less arcane prospect.

Type designer Christian Schwartz specializes in custom-made typefaces for publications and corporate identities. Among his recent commissions is the typeface Guardian Egyptian, which he designed with Paul Barnes for *The Guardian* newspaper.

The Guardian's recent shift in format from broadsheet to the smaller Berliner size initiated an entire redesign. Mark Porter, the newspaper's creative director, sought a new typeface with which to anchor his design. "The original plan was to adapt, rather than completely change, the design of the paper, and Paul Barnes brought me into the project to draw a very faithful revival of Neue Haas Grotesk to replace the Helvetica they had been using," says Schwartz. As the project evolved, Haas Grotesk fell by the wayside and the designers ended up collaborating on an entire suite of related faces. With just over 200 fonts, the Guardian family is one of the most ambitious custom type programs ever commissioned by a newspaper.

"Our initial work was on an elegant serif family to be used alongside the Haas Grotesk," says Schwartz. Porter was not convinced that two families were a comfortable match, however, and asked to see some tests for a new sans serif font. Barnes looked back to 1815, when the first face with slab serifs was invented. He decided to see what would happen if he drew an Egyptian, then trimmed the serifs off to get the sans—the same path that the very first sans serifs had taken. The Egyptian was planned as a "missing link"— an evolutionary step that would help the designer move from serif to sans, and that would not be used in the paper—but it quickly emerged as a clear favorite for both headlines and text.

"Our biggest influence was the Egyptian faces cast by London foundries in the mid-19th century," says Schwartz. What makes it feel more contemporary and elegant than the original faces, however, are new additions such as its weight contrast and the fact that the serifs are wedge-shaped, rather than simple slabs.

A newspaper font needs to work in many different situations, from attention-grabbing headlines, to legible text. Usually, type designers are able to test their designs for problems by running them through the paper's presses on the paper stock but, because the new presses for the Berliner format were not ready, and the stock for various sections had not yet been selected, the designers had to draw four grades of the text and agate families from which the printers would select the best one right before launching.

The best compliment that can be paid to a designer of typefaces for a newspaper is that it is invisible. As Barnes says, "I want people to feel 'that's interesting' on the first day and, by the third, be reading the news again."

Guardian Egyptian typeface
Designed by Christian
Schwartz and Paul Barnes.

Simon Schama:
America will never
be the same again

G2 Page 8

Lady Macbeth,
four-letter needle-
work and learning
from Cate Blanchett.
Judi Dench in her prime
G2, page 22

Chris Patten:
How the Tories
lost the plot

This Section Page 32

Amy Jenkins:
The me generation
is now in charge

G2 Page 2

£0.60

Monday 12.09.05
Published
in London and
Manchester
guardian.co.uk

theguardian

Backlash over Blair's school revolution

City academy plans condemned by ex-education secretary Morris

An acceleration of plans to reform state education, including the speeding up of the creation of the independently funded city academy schools, will be announced today by Tony Blair.

But the increasingly controversial nature of the policy was highlighted when the former education secretary Estelle Morris accused the government of "serial meddling" in secondary education.

In an article in tomorrow's Education Guardian she writes: "Another round of structural change won't by itself achieve universally high standards. Worse than that it could be a distraction. In five years' time, whose children will be going to these new academies? Will choice and market forces once again squeeze out the children of the disadvantaged?"

Today, the prime minister will say: "It is not government edict that is determining the fate of city academies, but parent power. Parents are choosing city academies, and that is good enough for me."

He will also set out the future of local

education authorities as "commissioners of education and champions of standards", rather than direct providers.

The academies replace failing schools, normally on new sites, in challenging inner-city areas. The number of academies will rise to between 40 and 50 by next September. This month 10 city academies started, bringing the total to 27, and Mr Blair will insist the government is on target to reach 200 by 2010. City academies have proved to be among the most hotly debated aspects of his public sector reforms. The Commons education select committee has criticised them as divisive and teaching union leaders have also denounced the expansion of an "unproven" scheme.

However, this will not deter Mr Blair who will point out that in the last academic year the proportion of pupils receiving five good GCSEs in city academies rose by 8 per cent, four times the national average.

Patrick Wintour and Rebecca Smithers

Bad'day mate Aussies lose their grip

Shane Warne at the Oval yesterday. Sport **»** Photograph: Kieran Doherty/Reuters

---

UK link to terror snatches

The United Nations is investigating the CIA's use of British airports when abducting terrorism suspects and flying them to prisons around the world where they are alleged to have been tortured. The inquiry, led by Martin Scheinin, a special rapporteur from the UN Commission on Human Rights, comes as an investigation by the Guardian reveals the full extent of the British logistical support. Aircraft used in the secret operations have flown into the UK at least 210 times since the September 11 terror attacks. Foreign Office officials have denied all knowledge of the

secret flights, telling MPs on the foreign affairs select committee that the ministry has "not granted any permissions for the use of UK territory or air space", and suggesting to the Guardian that it was "just a conspiracy theory" Privately, Ministry of Defence officials admit that they are aware of the flights, and that they have decided to turn a blind eye. "It is not a matter for the MoD," said one. "The aircraft use our airfields. We don't ask any questions. They just happen to be behind the wire."

Ian Cobain and Richard Norton-Taylor

13»

Column five
The shape of things to come

Alan Rusbridger

Welcome to the Berliner Guardian. No, we won't go on calling it that for long, and yes, it's an inelegant name.

We tried many alternatives, related either to size or to the European origins of the format. In the end, "the Berliner" stuck. But in a short time we hope we can revert to being simply the Guardian.

Many things about today's paper are different.

Starting with the most obvious, the page size is smaller. We believe the format combines the convenience of a tabloid with the sensibility of a broadsheet. Next most conspicuously, we have changed the paper's titlepiece and headline fonts. Gone is the striking 80s David Hillman design – adapted over the years – which mixed Garamond, Miller and Helvetica fonts. In their place is a new font, Guardian Egyptian, which is, we hope, elegant, intelligent and highly legible.

The next difference you may notice is colour. The paper is printed on state-of-the-art MAN Roland ColorMan presses, which give colour on every page – something that sets us apart from every other national newspaper. The effect will be to give greater emphasis and power to our photography and, we hope, make the whole paper a touch less forbidding than it sometimes may have seemed in the past.

G2 has also shrunk: it is now a full colour, stapled news magazine with newspaper deadlines. Sport has expanded into its own section – at least 12 pages every day, again in full colour.

As the week progresses you'll notice further changes. There are one or two new sections. There will be new columnists, both in G1 and G2 – most notably the pre-eminent commentator Simon Jenkins, who joins us from the Times to write on Wednesdays and Fridays.

Continued on page 2 »

National	Law	International	Financial
Police chief blames Orangemen for riots	**Judges may block deportations**	**Israeli troops leave Gaza after 38 years**	**Sky's Premiership rights under threat**
More than 2,000 police officers and soldiers clashed with loyalists in Belfast in the worst riots for more than a decade. The violence erupted after a small Orange Order parade was rerouted by fewer than 100 metres away from Catholic homes. Hugh Orde, Northern Ireland chief constable, accused Orangemen of taking part in and stoking up the riots, which spread to Ballymena, Antrim, Carrickfergus, Larne, Ballyclare, Glengormley and Ahoghill. More than 30 police and soldiers were injured as rioters used automatic weapons, petrol bombs and blast bombs to attack the security forces, who responded with 450 baton rounds. **3»**	The government faces a confrontation with judges over its attempts to deport terrorist suspects to Middle Eastern and north African countries with poor human rights records. Four appeal court judges who may have to decide whether deportations can go ahead have told the Guardian they will refuse to rubberstamp the UK's human rights deals with countries such as Jordan and Algeria. Despite being urged by the home secretary to respect the country-to-country agreements, the judges say they **15»** will demand evidence that the assurances are "worth the paper they're written on".	Israel lowered its flag in the Gaza Strip for the last time yesterday as the government declared an end to 38 years of occupation and troops withdrew from demolished Jewish settlements. The last troops were expected to leave overnight. Palestinian leaders described it as a "liberation", but said Israeli controls on border crossings and other restrictions maintained the occupation. Thousands of Palestinians gathered on roads leading to the settlements, ready to storm the rubble once the last troops were gone. A 12-year- **17»** old boy was seriously wounded by gunfire from an Israeli tank still guarding the settlements.	BSkyB's 13-year monopoly over live broadcasts of Premier League football games is under immediate threat. Media regulator Ofcom has told the European Commission it should force whoever holds the Premiership TV rights to sell a number of games to rival broadcasters. A separate regulatory plan under consideration in Brussels could see individual broadcasters limited to 50% of the live games put up for sale. The League, meanwhile, is resisting all attempts to remove its "exclusivity premium," arguing **26»** that clubs' finances will be undermined. The current rights deal expires in 2007.

Bigger isn't always better...

Writing

Writing not only provides a way for designers to explain and promote their work, but also is an important tool for helping to understand problems in ways that can inform design solutions. Thinking through writing differs qualitatively from thinking through designing. Articulating thoughts in a linear fashion where elements are examined sequentially can help to point out logical problems with an approach or help define a narrative sequence for presenting ideas.

Designers are using writing as a tool to examine and improve their own work, a means to create their own or to supplement the given content for a project, and to contribute to the body of critical and historical inquiry about the discipline they practice. It seems as if there are more designers writing than ever before; but it may be just that their words are more visible due to a proliferation of new vehicles for design writing and criticism. Printed periodicals such as *Eye* continue to play a vital role within the community by presenting carefully researched articles on issues and new thinking in graphic design, while also reexamining historical work and bringing to light the kinds of things that have been overlooked or undervalued. Other magazines, such as *Grafik*, which appear more frequently, focus on news-driven stories, reviews, and designers' opinions on topical issues.

In addition to these traditional publishing formats, a new platform for a new type of design writing has emerged. Perhaps the most important recent development in design writing is the emergence of blogs— on-line forums in which sanctioned authors post entries or short essays to which anyone can append comments. Blogs serve many functions: they provide designers a way of airing their ideas and gathering quick feedback. They also provide geographically dispersed designers with an immediate means of discussing the various issues confronting the profession. *Design Observer*, for example, is a blog founded in 2003 by William Drentell and Jessica Helfand of the publishing and design firm Winterhouse, along with Michael Bierut, partner at Pentagram, and design critic Rick Poynor. With 250,000 site visits each month, the blog provides a viable forum for debate about various aspects of visual culture that range from the arcane to the practical. Because a successful blog entry is one that generates a lot of comments, they have given birth to a new form of writing, in which provocation plays a heightened role and embedded links are harnessed for their explicatory power. The unedited and unsupported comments tend to develop (and devolve) along more than one theme, resulting in an often-confusing reading experience, but the blog's ability to monitor the pulse of the design community on a given topic at a given moment is a valuable addition to the spectrum of tools available for research and writing about design.

Eye magazine cover
Designed by Esterson Associates. *Eye* was founded by Rick Poyner and is now edited by John L. Walters.

Design Observer page
Blog founded by Michael Bierut, Bill Drentell, Jessica Helfand, and Rick Poynor.

Software design

It is only since computers became the dominant method for making design that designers have lost touch with their tools. Software packages have replaced traditional tools, the mechanics of which were easier to access and adapt. Today, however, many designers are discovering new possibilities and ways of working through the creation of their own software.

These applications are rarely built from scratch but usually based on existing software such as Adobe Illustrator. Most designers start by writing code to solve specific problems or achieve specific effects. Often, they discover that other designers face similar problems and need similar solutions. By sharing code, they invite these other designers to modify it. But why would designers choose to help the competition by giving away something they have worked hard to create? Because often the results of such additions are bigger and richer than the code creator could have achieved or even imagined by themselves.

In this open-source spirit, the Dutch type foundry LettError has created RoboFab, a whole library of code that they offer for free that helps to eliminate repetitive tasks from the font design and production process. Erik van Blokland, Tal Leming, and Just van Rossum (The RoboFab Consortium) had been working on utilities to make FontLab easier to script and use. In an effort to combine, rather than duplicate efforts, they initiated RoboFab. Type designer Ben Kiel describes the result of their labors: "Like a set of Lego, RoboFab gives a type designer building blocks for making useful tools."

Of course, not all designers choose to give away the code they've worked so hard to create. Many designers have discovered that the software they've created has commercial value. Design and special effects studio The Orphanage now sells a series of software packages for creating film effects. Magic Bullet, for example, is a powerful finishing tool that makes materials originated in digital video exhibit all the characteristics of celluloid film.

In the future, there will likely be more designers who make their own software and modify existing software. The current generation of emerging designers has grown up working almost exclusively with computers, and feels comfortable with adapting and creating software. At the same time, as

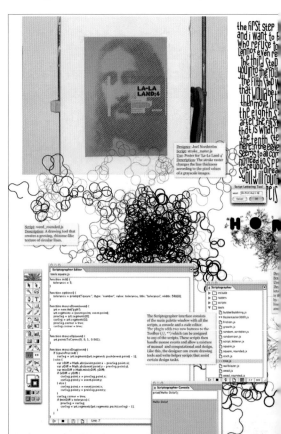

the limitations of packaged software and the homogeneity of their end products become increasingly apparent, more and more designers will want to take back control of their tools as a way to reintroduce individuality and texture to their work.

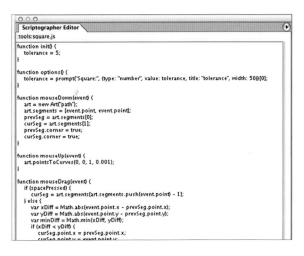

```
000
Scriptographer Editor
:tools:square.js
function init() {
    tolerance = 5;
}

function options() {
    tolerance = prompt("Square:", {type: "number", value: tolerance, title: "tolerance", width: 50})[0];
}

function mouseDown(event) {
    art = new Art("path");
    art.segments = [event.point, event.point];
    prevSeg = art.segments[0];
    curSeg = art.segments[1];
    prevSeg.corner = true;
    curSeg.corner = true;
}

function mouseUp(event) {
    art.pointsToCurves(0, 0, 1, 0.001);
}

function mouseDrag(event) {
    if (spacePressed) {
        curSeg = art.segments[art.segments.push(event.point) - 1];
    } else {
        var xDiff = Math.abs(event.point.x - prevSeg.point.x);
        var yDiff = Math.abs(event.point.y - prevSeg.point.y);
        var minDiff = Math.min(xDiff, yDiff);
        if (xDiff < yDiff) {
            curSeg.point.x = prevSeg.point.x;
            curSeg.point.y = event.point.y;
```

Below: Scriptographer poster

Jürg Lehni has created a new kind of software to run a new kind of printer that follows vector graphic paths. To run his Graffiti Robot, Lehni created a program that converts Adobe Illustrator files into digital paths for the robotic spray can to follow. He calls this program Scriptographer. This poster for an exhibition on Scriptographer shows all the designs that have been created using adaptations of Lehni's original piece of code.

Above: Scriptographer interface

Designed by Jürg Lehni.

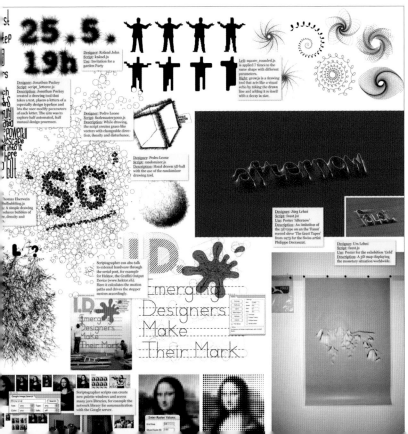

Mise-en-scène

"BITE" is spelled out in tubes of white neon light. Receding along multiple lines of perspective are other streaks of typographic information made up of the dots and lines spawned by LED display matrixes and cathode rays. They burn through the darkness with their orange light. Beyond them is a background that keeps shifting beyond your reach like the back wall of the Narnian-wardrobe. It is deeply dark but shot with sudden explosions of hot light, color-saturated with a blown glass richness, and trails of blurred discs like the reflections of billboard lights on a wet road. The trails disintegrate into delicate filaments, codes of dots and dashes, and finally hazy vapor. Further still into the distance of this surreal mise-en-scène is the underside of an airplane wing searing through eerily moonlit clouds. This poster is for one of The Barbican's International Theater Events and has been created by the British design firm Why Not Associates. Despite the bright-colored verve of the poster the world barely contained by its edges is a disturbing and vertiginous one. The extreme dimensionality of the composition plunges you down through layers and slides you sideways across tilted planes. There seems at times little for the viewer to cling to. But despite its proximity to chaos, the design has a visual rhythm to it, the subtlest of grids, and the confidence born of immaculate typographic craftsmanship, that holds image and text in a tense relationship, atmosphere, and emotion in measured check.

The term mise-en-scène means, literally, "put in the scene" and originates in the theater. For film, it has a broader meaning, and refers to almost everything that goes into the composition of the shot, including the composition itself: framing, movement of the camera and characters, lighting, set design, and general visual environment. For designers an involvement in the making of things, and the composition of scenes using real objects has a particular resonance right now. Partly this is because many designers are uninspired by the slick surfaces of software programs, frustrated by sitting in front of computer screens all day, and are enjoying rediscovering the textures, rough edges and shadows inherent in 3D forms.

Dimensionality is an important component of the Why Not Associates' work, whether through motion and time in their commercials, experimental films, and video pieces, or through space in their multimedia compositions, exhibitions, or the intricate mise-en-scènes they construct for print work. It is also evident in the work of Stefan Sagmeister. His poster to promote the Adobe Design Achievement Award, for example, depicts a designer (Matthias Ernstberger)

"Barbican International Theater Event" poster
Designed by Why Not Associates.

BITE:00
BARBICAN INTERNATIONAL THEATRE EVENT

BARBICAN INTERNATIONAL THEATRE EVENT

MAY > OCTOBER

THEATRE   DANCE   MUSIC

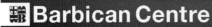 **Barbican Centre**
Box Office 020 7638 8891 Bkg fee (9am-8pm) daily
www.barbican.org.uk

creating the shape of a trophy out of paper coffee cups. To produce this shot, Sagmeister needed a studio with 30ft (9m) ceilings and scaffolding to enable the photographer to be high enough to capture the scene. He had a wooden floor constructed and then arranged 2,500 filled coffee cups.

The Swiss designer Martin Woodtli, a one-time intern of Sagmeister's, is also interested in the qualitative difference between designing in space and designing on the screen. For a poster to announce an exhibition about the interplay between objects and light, he decided to create an installation incorporating the exhibition's themes—shadows, transparency, and reflection in its very fabric. He shot the installation using a trade camera and documented the process of making. Such explorations of form represent a renewed interest on the part of designers in the integrity of the hand-crafted, the physical, and the real.

Next page: Adobe Design Achievement Awards poster Designed by Stefan Sagmeister.

Right: Identity sequence for a Virgin conference Designed by Why Not Associates.

2003
Adobe
DESIGN ACHIEVEMENT
AWARDS
CALL for ENTRIES

GETTING AN "A"
ON THIS PROJECT
COULD GET YOU $5000
AND A TRIP TO CHICAGO

Accepting entries
from APRIL 1
through
MAY 15, 2003.

Adobe

OPEN TO FULL TIME VISUAL ARTS STUDENTS
attending accredited U.S., U.K., and Canadian
(excluding the Province of Quebec)
institutions of higher education and who meet the eligibility
requirements described in the rules.

Portfolios

"Graphic design is for saying a certain thing to a certain group in a certain setting, so nicely that other groups get interested and other meanings arise," says David Reinfurt, founder of ORG, a design practice in New York. This approach to design, which begins with a certain point of specificity and situation, but grows in unpredictable directions through the different ways in which it is read and understood, is one that absorbs some of today's most thoughtful designers.

Each of the studios featured on the following pages was asked to submit projects that consciously engage with and speak to a particular community. Sometimes, a community is united by shared passion, such as the readers of Vince Frost's literary magazine *Zembla*, or the viewers of Scott Stowell's short films about jazz legends. Sometimes, designers incorporate the community into the work itself, such as COMA's sugar packaging that features quotes by people who were asked to "describe something sweet," or John Morgan's typographic installations for the BBC in London that use the words of local residents. Sometimes, a project speaks to people who live in the same place, such as Base's work for the Belgian National Theater, or David Reinfurt's design of an identity to connect nine arts venues in Long Island City. Conversely, the audience can be globally dispersed, such as the viewers of barbara says' identity system for Portugal at the 2004 Venice Architecture Biennial, or the tourist consumers of Kerr|Noble's series of packages for the retailer Liberty, which include illustrated jokes about obscure English traditions.

The 15 studios in this section work on both local projects and for international clients or clients with international audiences. While in no way representative of graphic design as a whole, this selection of studios offers a broad range of insights into contemporary graphic design practice from the perspective of designers in the US, Portugal, Brazil, France, the Netherlands, the UK, Australia, Slovenia, Switzerland, and Belgium.

The studios range in scale from international advertising powerhouse Wieden+Kennedy, whose work is broadcast through multiple channels, to Radovan Jenko, who specializes in creating one type of artifact—posters—for clients in just two cities in Slovenia.

Regardless of size, all of the featured studios share a sensitivity to the needs, desires, and intelligence of their audiences. This may seem like a prerequisite for engaging in design work, but, in fact, it is surprisingly rare. Many designers take their clients' word for what their constituents want rather than attempting to discover for themselves. Work that is made with real people in mind leaves itself open to new interpretations, evolution, and distortion. To some designers, the lack of control implicit in allowing for change and engaging with one's audiences during the design process is disconcerting; to others it is liberating and, as the Swiss designer Martin Woodtli says, "real."

Kerr|Noble

Traditional Inuit maps were 3D objects made from wood, designed to be felt rather than looked at. Their edges could be "read" with the fingertips on a dark night in a kayak, and they were more resistant to weather than a chart made of paper. Amelia Noble, one half of British design team Kerr|Noble, points out these objects as "brilliant information design," and an exemplar of graphic design's purpose that, in her view, is: "To make life easier for people."

After meeting as students at the Royal College of Art during the mid-1990s, Noble and Frith Kerr set up a consultancy based in London. Like the Inuit maps, Kerr|Noble's work contains an extra dimension not found in most graphic design—an unexpected layer of information that both surprises and delights the audience. This ability to see beyond the ordinary has earned them respect within the international design community and repeat commissions from some of London's foremost clients, including: The Natural History Museum, The Architecture Foundation, Tate Modern, The Serpentine Gallery, The Crafts Council, and The Design Museum.

While their research-rich approach is sought out more regularly by cultural organizations than by commercial concerns, they are no strangers to design's role in selling units. In fact, they are so good at this that when they developed a range of food packaging for the department store Liberty, certain items had completely sold out even before they'd had a chance to get samples for their portfolio.

Kerr|Noble try to find out as much as they can about the audience for a particular project. "The end user is the one we really want to please," they say. They think that, on the whole, the public is not credited with enough intelligence. "A client can be reserved about how far to push something, worrying that their message won't come across," Noble explains. "But, actually, the public is very receptive to new things— things that look different and are actually interesting." As long as the duo are confident that what they are doing will communicate— which is, after all, their job—they like to add what they call "intriguing moments"— curiosities and stories that add depth to someone's experience of a piece of their graphic design.

One of Kerr|Noble's preferred methods of connecting with an audience is through storytelling. When you unscrew the lid of a jelly jar Kerr|Noble designed for Liberty, you'll find a comment there about how it's considered impolite not to take one's hat off indoors. It's part of a series of illustrated jokes about curious English traditions applied across the range of food packaging, conceived with the foreign visitor to London firmly in mind. Such eccentricity doesn't always gel with the client's initial perspective and Kerr|Noble say they spend a lot of time convincing their clients to let them: "Go the extra mile to make things happen."

The energy required for such persistence comes from a compulsion to experiment. As they put it, "It's in our blood to keep pushing things and to make new creative challenges for ourselves." Each new project brings with it the excitement of a new context. "There's opportunity in anything in graphic design."

PETER ANDERSSON
LENA BERGSTRÖM
SARA BERNER
THOMAS BERNSTRAND
CLAESSON KOIVISTO RUNE
BJÖRN DAHLSTRÖM
MONICA FÖRSTER & FRONT
MIA E. GÖRANSSON
ANGELICA GUSTAFSSON
MATTI KLENELL
ANNA KRAITZ
JONAS LINDVALL
& ANDERS LJUNGBERG
ANNA KRISTINA LUNDBERG
MÄRTEN MEDBO
GUSTAF NORDENSKIÖLD
INGEGERD RÁMAN
KJELL RYLANDER
GUNNEL SAHLIN & SALDO
PER SUNDBERG
PIA TÖRNELL UGLYCUTE
ANNA VON SCHEWEN

TIMBER TYPE

AÅAABZZCCDEFGHIJKLMN
NOÖPQQRRSTUVWZXYZ:.,

**"Beauty And The Beast"
poster, gallery guide,
and font**

"When we worked on 'Beauty And The Beast'—a show about Swedish design for the Crafts Council in London— we decided that the last thing we wanted to do was look at Swedish design," say Kerr|Noble. The designers spent three-and-a-half weeks of the month allotted to them for the preparation of design concepts in researching and thinking about Swedish people, habits, and weather. They discovered that most Swedes have a second home in forests, and that tree cutting is a big part of their lives, land, and landscape. The font that they developed, Timber Type, came from the idea of cutting simple log shapes with an axe

C

BEAUTY
AND
THE
BEAST

New Swedish Design

18 November 2004—6 February 2005
Crafts Council Gallery. Free Entry.

Crafts Council, 44a Pentonville Road, London N1 9BY
Tuesday to Saturday 11am—6pm, Sunday 2—6pm
Shop and Resource Centre. Closed Monday.
Disabled Access. Three minutes from Angel Tube
Telephone 020 7278 7700 www.craftscouncil.org.uk
The Crafts Council strives to beat equal opportunities employer
Registered charity number 280956 Design: Kerr|Noble Photo: Ed Park

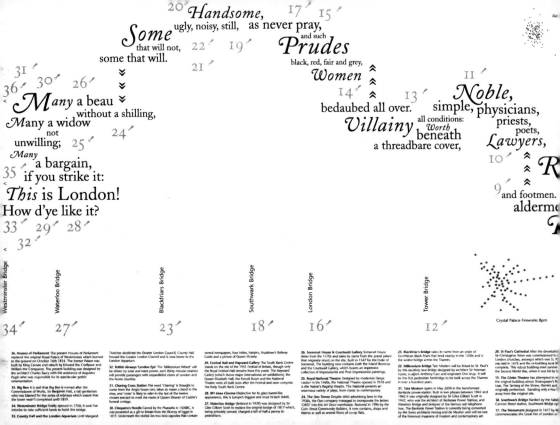

Handsome,
ugly, noisy, still, as never pray,
Some
that will not, and such
some that will. *Prudes*
Women black, red, fair and grey,
bedaubed all over.

Many a beau
without a shilling,
Many a widow
not
unwilling;
Many
a bargain,
if you strike it:
This is London!
How d'ye like it?

Villainy *Worth* beneath
all conditions:
a threadbare cover,

Noble,
simple, physicians,
priests,
poets,
Lawyers,

and footmen.
alderme[n]

Crystal Palace Fireworks 8pm

Westminster Bridge   Waterloo Bridge   Blackfriars Bridge   Southwark Bridge   London Bridge   Tower Bridge

36. Houses of Parliament The present Houses of Parliament replaced the original Royal Palace of Westminster which burned to the ground on October 16th 1834. The former Palace was built by King Canute and rebuilt by Edward the Confessor and William the Conqueror. The present building was designed by the architect Charles Barry with the assistance of Augustus Pugin who was responsible for its spectacular gothic ornamentation.

35. Big Ben It is said that Big Ben is named after the Commissioner of Works, Sir Benjamin Hall, a tall gentleman who was blamed for the series of mishaps which meant that the tower wasn't completed until 1859.

34. Westminster Bridge Originally opened in 1750. It took five lotteries to raise sufficient funds to build the bridge.

33. County Hall and the London Aquarium Until Margaret Thatcher abolished the Greater London Council, County Hall housed the Greater London Council and is now home to the London Aquarium.

32. British Airways 'London Eye' The 'Millennium Wheel' will be driven by solar and wave power, each thirty minute rotation will provide passengers with unparalleled views of London and the home counties.

31. Charing Cross Station The word 'Charing' is thought to come from the Anglo-Saxon *cerr*, taken to mean a bend in the river, and 'cross' is likely to refer to the last of the twelve crosses erected to mark the route of Queen Eleanor of Castile's funeral cortege.

30. Festival Hall and Hayward Gallery The South Bank Centre stands on the site of the 1951 Festival of Britain, though only the Royal Festival Hall remains from this event. The Hayward Gallery (which shows major international art exhibitions), the Queen Elizabeth Hall, the Purcell Room and the National Theatre were all built soon after the Festival and now comprise the lively South Bank Centre.

29. ... several newspapers, four bibles, hairpins, Bradshaw's Railway Guide and a picture of Queen Victoria.

28. BFI Imax Cinema Distinctive for its glass barrel-like appearance, this is Europe's biggest and most hi-tech IMAX.

27. Waterloo Bridge (finished in 1939) was designed by Sir Giles Gilbert Scott to replace the original bridge of 1817 which, being privately owned, charged a toll of half a penny to pedestrians.

26. Somerset House & Courtauld Gallery Somerset House dates from the 1770s and takes its name from the grand palace that originally stood on the site, built in 1547 for the Duke of Somerset. The building now contains both the Inland Revenue and the Courtauld Gallery, which boasts an impressive collection of Impressionist and Post-Impressionist paintings.

25. Royal National Theatre Designed by modernist Denys Lasdun in the 1960s, the National Theatre opened in 1976 and is the Nation's flagship theatre. The National presents an enormous variety of plays, from classic to contemporary.

24. The Oxo Tower Despite strict advertising laws in the 1930s, the Oxo company managed to incorporate the letters 'OXO' into this Art Deco warehouse. Restored in 1996 by the Coin Street Community Builders, it now contains, shops and bistros as well as several floors of co-op flats.

23. Blackfriars' Bridge takes its name from an order of Dominican Black Friars that lived nearby in the 1280s and is the widest bridge across the Thames.

22. Millennium Bridge Tate Modern will be linked to St. Paul's by this exciting new bridge designed by architect Sir Norman Foster, sculptor Anthony Caro and engineers Ove Arup. It will be the first pedestrian footbridge to be built across the Thames in over a hundred years.

21. Tate Modern opens in May 2000 in the transformed Bankside power-station. Built in two phases between 1947 and 1963 it was originally designed by Sir Giles Gilbert Scott in 1947, who was the architect of Battersea Power Station, and Waterloo bridge and designer of the famous red telephone box. The Bankside Power Station is currently being converted by the Swiss architects Herzog and de Meuron and will be one of the foremost museums of modern and contemporary art.

20. St Paul's Cathedral After the devasta[tion] ... Sir Christopher Wren was commissioned to [rebuild] London churches, amongst which was St. [Paul's]. ... was laid in 1675 and the re-building took th[irty years] to complete. This robust building even surviv[ed] the Second World War, when it was hit by b[ombs].

19. The Globe Theatre has attempted to re-[create] the original building where Shakespeare's *Ro[meo and Juliet]*, *Lear*, *The Taming of the Shrew*, *Hamlet* and [others were] originally performed. Standing only a few [feet] away from the original site.

18. Southwark Bridge Pushed by the Italia[n builders] Cannon Street station, Southwark Bridge op[ened] ...

17. The Monument designed in 1677 by [Wren] commemorates the Great Fire of London [of 1666]

Warrants, bailiffs, bills UNPAID, laundresses ...d; that rob and shoot men, men, carts. and wheelbarrows Coaches, arts, MECHANIC trades, Bubbles, empty; insides outsides, Showy tempt ye, Gaudy things enough TO together, mixed Streets unpleasant churches, Houses, in all weather; Prisons, palaces contiguous, Gates, the a bridge, Thames irriguous.

8 1 2 6 5 4 7 3

6PM ON THE 6TH OF NOVEMBER 1999

...n Pudding Lane in September 1666.

...dge Lane in the 18th century, London Bridge was ... over-crossing. The current bridge built in 1973 a... exist on this site including one built in 1176 ...d many houses and shops and even a chapel. ...he famous residents were Holbein and Hogarth ...eads of Thomas More and William Wallace, ...played on spikes at either end of the bridge.

...gate Fish Market Until its relocation to the Isle ..., a fish market had existed on this site since ...he Old Billingsgate Fish Market building which ...5 was renovated by architect Richard Rogers in

...Before it arrived at its final resting place on the ...5 Belfast was active from the Second World War

(including the D-Day landings) until the end of the Korean war.

13. The Tower of London originally began life as one of three castles belonging to William the Conqueror and subsequently added to by successive monarchs. In its time the compound has housed elephants, lions, eagles, mountain cats, an elephant and a bear as well as many famous prisoners including Lady Jane Grey, Sir Thomas More, Thomas Cromwell, Elizabeth I, Sir Walter Raleigh, Guy Fawkes and more recently Rudolph Hess, Hitler's deputy. The Tower is perhaps most famous for containing the Crown Jewels and the site where two of Henry VIII's wives were executed.

12. Tower Bridge was the work of two men: Horace Jones, responsible for the mock-medieval stone exterior and engineer John Wolfe-Barry who designed the distinctive bascules that are raised allowing tall ships to pass. In its first year of operation (1894), Tower Bridge was raised an average of sixteen times a

day, and even today, the bridge is still raised once a day.

11. St Katharine's Dock in 1820 the development of St Katharine's Dock was announced amidst public outcry. Within a month 1250 houses were demolished, and eleven thousand people made homeless. The docks stayed in use until 1968 and were the first of their land to be redeveloped in 1973.

10. Butler's Wharf Once one of London's busiest docks, Butler's Wharf was renovated in the 1980s (just over a century after it was built) and now houses luxury flats, speciality wine and food shops and restaurants.

9. The Design Museum was the brainchild of design gurus Terence Conran and Stephen Bayley, and is the only museum in the world dedicated entirely to housing icons of modern design.

8. Canary Wharf standing at 812 ft, with its recognisable

triangular peak, dominates the London skyline. Built in 1991 by Canadian property developers Olympia and York, it is not only the tallest building in Britain but the first skyscraper in the world to be clad in stainless steel (27,500 tonnes). The building derives its name from the Wharf's original use as a receiver of cargoes from the Canary Islands in the nineteenth century.

7. The Cutty Sark is famous for completing the annual clipper's race in 1871 from Shanghai to London in a record one hundred and seven days, was the last of the great tea clippers. The clipper spent the rest of her life transporting cargoes of tea from India and China and wool and grain from Australia.

6. Greenwich Foot Tunnel was constructed in 1903 and links Greenwich to the Isle of Dogs. It takes 4 minutes to walk through.

5. Royal Naval College It's magnificent façade, the combined work of architects Wren, Hawksmoor and Vanbrugh, has meant

that it is often used for film shoots. However, its original use was as a hospital for disabled sailors commissioned by Queen Mary in 1696. Under increasing allegations of corruption, the building was handed over to the Royal Navy in 1873.

4. The Queen's House & National Maritime Museum The Queen's House, sandwiched between two wings of the Royal Naval College, is modelled on the Palladian villas that so inspired its architect, Inigo Jones. Dating from 1615, the house, built for Queen Anne of Denmark, is sumptuously decorated with paintings by Titian, Rubens, Raphael and Van Dyck. The National Maritime Museum boasts a large selection of naval artefacts including the uniform in which Nelson died at Trafalgar.

3. Old Royal Observatory marks the point of 0° longitude, where Eastern and Western Hemispheres divide. Though the Observatory was founded by Charles II and designed by Christopher Wren) in 1675 to investigate a way of measuring

longitude, it was almost a century later that clockmaker John Harrison finally succeeded in Yorkshire in 1772.

2. Reuters Building The global news agency Reuters began life in 1849 as a continental pigeon post. Its London headquarters are now housed in this building designed in 1989 by Richard Rogers.

1. Millennium Dome Made from Teflon and fibreglass and supported by twelve steel masts, the Dome is large enough to hold thirteen Royal Albert Halls, tall enough to accommodate Nelson's Column and has enough strength to hold a jumbo jet. The Dome is estimated to cost £758 million and will house a stage, with live show, surrounded by fourteen thematic zones, each with a different sponsor.

Poem: 'A Description of London' by John Bancks, 1738
Produced by Farm for Channel Four Television Corporation
Design: Kerri Noble

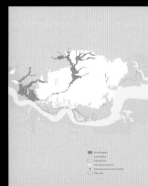

THURROCK:
A
VISIONARY
BRIEF
IN
THE
THAMES
GATEWAY

"Thurrock: A Visionary Brief in the Thames Gateway"
The General Public Agency (GPA) wanted to create a briefing pack that would entice international artists, architects, and cultural figures to brainstorm and inform a brief intended to become a successful model for national and international regeneration schemes. Kerr|Noble made it in the form of a box that would function as a mini-bureau. GPA had already commissioned three artists to make inspiration pieces for the briefing pack—they produced a set of postcards, Polaroid photographs, and a hardback graphic novel that presented a fantasy vision of Thurrock in 2015. Kerr|Noble entered into a productive dialog of formats with each of these artists, producing booklets that corresponded in size and spirit to the artists' works.

This Artangel exhibition by Kutlug Ataman, located in an old mail sorting office on London's Oxford Street was about the inhabitants of Küba, an impossible-to-locate "underground" community in the center of Istanbul. When asked to produce graphic materials to accompany the exhibition (advertising, explanatory guides, postcards, invitations, internal and external signage for the sorting office, and a Web site), Kerr|Noble responded to the subject matter and the raw character of the building. They used the materials and low-tech production methods they imagined would be available to the inhabitants of Küba. This included printing publicity on 42,000 cheap plastic bags that were distributed to newsagents, printing the exhibition guide on recycled stock, and including a map that looked as if someone had drawn it for you, and applying the signage to the building using vinyl stencils and layering on top of the existing graffiti.

KÜBA

Kutlug Ataman

22nd March – 7th May 2005
The Sorting Office,
21 – 31 New Oxford Street, London WC1
www.kuba.org.uk

Küba

Symposium: Where is Küba?

Opening Times at The Sorting Office

Publication

Admission Free

Location

Access

Λrtangel

www.kuba.org.uk

I WANT TO STAY HERE ALWAYS

Left: General Public Agency identity

Kerr|Noble worked closely with General Public Agency (GPA)—an organization that provides programs that help to animate and sustain public space improvements—to create an ideology for GPA's new identity. As *The Independent* newspaper noted, "GPA wants new architecture and infrastructure to be grounded precisely in the values, creativity, and aspirations of local people and their environment." Responding to this, their solution was to construct a community-building tool that would collect images from the general public about the general public and ultimately for the general public. The copyright-free images were used on business cards, featured on the Web site, and e-mailed to subscribers each week.

Right: Import Export exhibition identity, graphics, and catalog

The British Council's traveling exhibition "Import Export" showcases 14 international designers/ teams who live and work in the UK. It aims to illuminate aspects of global exchange in design and the multicultural nature of the British design community. Kerr|Noble infused their design for the catalog with ideas of travel and dispersal, migration and movement. In order to show what the featured designers looked like, Kerr|Noble commissioned portraits. "They're quite severe," say the designers, "but they are also honest and provide a snapshot of a situation at a certain moment in time."

GENERAL PUBLIC

10 Stoney Street | London | SE1 9AD
T: +44 (0)20 7378 8365
F: +44 (0)20 7378 8366
mail@generalpublicagency.com
www.generalpublicagency.com

Clare Cumberlidge
GENERAL PUBLIC

10 Stoney Street | London | SE1 9AD
T: +44 (0)20 7378 8365
F: +44 (0)20 7378 8366
mail@generalpublicagency.com
www.generalpublicagency.com

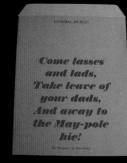

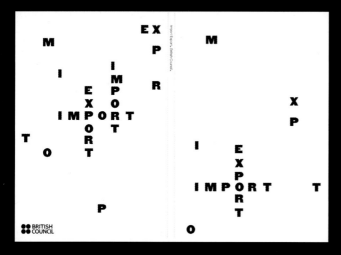

Left: Konstam café identity
Kerr|Noble's design of the café's identity and a set of souvenir cards emphasize the locality of the café and aim to make customers feel welcome. One postcard features lettering found on the window of the "solarium" next door, and hand-drawn maps point out local attractions such as a "secret garden" and "a nice church with benches outside." The star lettering used as a titling font throughout the identity was made especially for Konstam, a Polish family name of the owner's. Kerr|Noble covered one wall of the interior entirely in corkboard and commissioned the illustrator Ian Wright to create a stag out of gold drawing pins. The board provides a place for staff, regulars, and tourists to pin images, postcards, and even currency.

Vince Frost

"You can be anywhere in the world today and be designing," says Vince Frost, the senior creative director at Frost Design, founded in London and now based in Sydney. "There was a time only a few years ago when large corporations went to large design firms in their own cities," says Frost. "They don't do that anymore. They've learned that smaller organizations are much more hands-on and unique in their thinking and that, thanks to good e-mail connections, it's not necessary to be in the same country as the project." Frost, the consummate global designer, is currently working with clients in London, Beijing, Dubai, and Hong Kong.

Frost's conceptual photographic covers for *The Independent*'s Saturday magazine and his sculptural use of blocky typography in *Big* magazine in the 1990s won him awards and confirmed his status as a major player in editorial design. Among the many other projects his London studio was lauded for are the visually inventive newsletters for D&AD, portfolios for Magnum, stamps for the Royal Mail, TV advertising for BT, and the visual identity of *The Financial Times*' magazine.

Frost moved to Australia in 2004. For the first year he worked with Gary Emery on large-scale, strategy-heavy projects like branding, signage systems, and even the masterplan for a new ticketing system for public transport in Sydney. Frost now works under his own name and balances corporate problem-solving with cultural sector projects such as an identity for the Sydney Dance Company, magazines, film titles, and books. An interesting new project that straddles both commerce and culture is his design for a new film classification for Australia. The system applies to DVDs, posters, movies, and games, and represents exactly the kind of challenge that Frost relishes most.

"With everything we do here, we think about the end user, the person who is going to receive this thing," Frost says. "We constantly remind ourselves that this stuff is for people rather than our portfolios."

Sometimes, as in the case of *Ampersand*, the D&AD newsletter, the audience is other designers. "I was aware that this was going out to 3,000 designers—my peers. I wasn't just aware of the audience; I was intimidated by it because I knew how critical they could be." Frost designed the newsletter for nine years and, in the end, he admits, "it was fun."

Sometimes the end user is a client. "When you're designing an identity, a newsletter, or magazine for someone, it has to be done with them in mind. It's pointless designing something that they cannot access or update." Frost believes that his most successful work has come out of a successful collaboration with a client. "One where a client understands the benefit of what we can do; understands that we're both playful and intelligent, and determined at all costs to make this project or opportunity the best it can be."

"I like restrictions, too," says Frost. "When a client says something has to be A4, one-color, you have to use Helvetica, and there's no budget for images, I think, 'fantastic!' There's so much potential, even within those tight parameters. I hate it when other designers say to me, 'It's OK for you because you have such nice jobs.' There's such thing as nice jobs or bread-and-butter jobs. You just have to find a way to make each job great. I love miserable clients who have no money."

GRAND
Dance by Graeme Murphy
...with piano in mind

Sydney
Dance
Company

World Premiere Season 1–18 June 2005
Opera Theatre Sydney Opera House
Previews 28, 30, 31 May
Bookings: phone 9250 7777 sydneyoperahouse.com
Ticketek 9266 4800 Tickets from $29

"It is fabulous working with Graeme Murphy," says Frost of his ongoing collaboration with the choreographer and founder of the Sydney Dance Company. The Company's target audience is dance and classical music fanatics as well as the wider arts community. When asked to create an image for use on marketing collateral for a new piece called Grand, Frost wanted to capture the physicality of contemporary dance as well as the classical connotations of the grand piano, which was a theme of the piece's choreography. Frost's solution was to use typography that visually echoed the punched holes in old pianola sheets. He worked closely with costume designer Akira Isogawa, and photographer Stephen Ward.

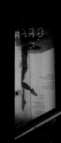

z have and z hold

Since the beginning of time human beings have collected objects

...well-considered collector of objects Peter Reeve is someone who... the human desire for beautiful things. An interior decorator by trade, he lives in... immaculately renovated terrace house in Surry Hills where it's apparent that... been built to display his objects, rather than the objects having been placed... Peter comments, "as a designer my advice to people is to make sure you feel it reflects you. It should be about how you feel, it's about what you like, it reflects your fascinations and your moods and the way you like to live." ...Peter's home, utilising natural light, open spaces and architectural form to highlight his collection of vases and sculptures. Each piece stands alone as testimony to his appreciation of objects, yet also works as a whole to offer a visual representation...

colour spectrum

jonathan bashett: colour spectrum

Jonathan Bashett re-defines the everyday in a very colourful way...

Frank le petit

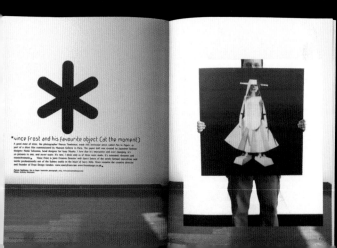

*vince frost and his favourite object (at the moment)

A good read of mine, the photographer Pierre Vondeous made this bestseller...

exhibitive

18 september to 31 october 2002

OBJECT GALLERY

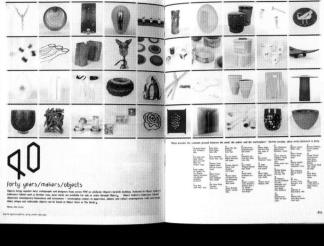

qo

forty years/makers/objects

sequeira:
same but different

Objective Collective magazine

The Object design center promotes and showcases the best of contemporary craft and new design in Australia. Looking to position themselves at the heart of Sydney's design community, the directors approached emeryfrost to help them create a bi-annual magazine. The result is *Objective Collective*, a snapshot of contemporary craft and design practice that takes place in a creative community in Sydney's Surry Hills district, with a special emphasis on people who collect design. emeryfrost designed a magazine they hoped would become a desirable object in its own right. It features a new typeface, Hex, by David Pidgeon, that Frost noticed was particularly 3D, as if "each letter was an object in itself."

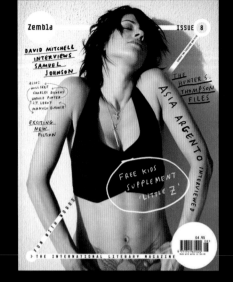

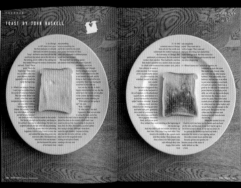

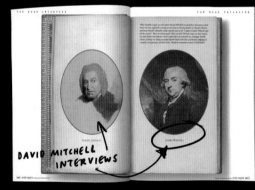

Little Z

> F U N   W I T H   W O R D S <

Left: *Zembla* magazine
Vince Frost art directs *Zembla* from Sydney, it is published in London, and then distributed around the world. *Zembla* is, according to its promotional material, "A literary magazine that people actually want to read." For Frost Design, it was an opportunity to create an entirely new magazine, to indulge a passion for typography, and to take the magazine's strap line—"fun with words"—as a modus operandi. Eschewing all precedents in the literary magazine genre, Frost took a freeform approach: a grid is used only when needed and typeface, size, and character are flexible.

Right and below: *Little Z* magazine
Little Z is an offshoot of *Zembla*, designed just for kids. This first edition appeared as a pullout in *Zembla* and uses illustration instead of photography to accompany articles. The fully fledged version will contain poems, games, competitions, and fun.

MACQUARIE BANK
2005 FINANCIAL REPORT

MACQUARIE
BANK

MACQUARIE BANK
INVESTOR OVERVIEW
YEAR ENDED 31 MARCH 2005

MACQUARIE BANK
RESULT ANNOUNCEMENT
YEAR ENDED 31 MARCH 2005

MACQUARIE BANK LIMITED ACN 008 583 542

COMA

In 1998, Swiss artist Cornelia Blatter and Dutch graphic designer Marcel Hermans joined forces to form design agency COMA, dividing their time between two studios—one in Amsterdam, the other in New York. They have discovered that collaboration improves the quality of their work. While they have expertise in different fields, they share a conceptual approach to designing and have found that discussion is always constructive.

It's essential for them both to feel an affinity with the content of a project, because their design emanates directly from the project's subject matter or, more precisely, from the germ of an idea they find within it. When they're doing an artist's book, for example, the design always comes out of a theme, a process, or a preoccupation they identify in the work of the artist. When they're doing a compendium or a catalog, the logistics of the project dictate the structure and the structure determines the esthetic. "Once the concept is decided upon," say COMA, "things like the choice of typeface, colors, and so on become just like adding a little seasoning to an amazing meal."

When they describe the books they design, to convey the concept, the construction, and the atmosphere in each example, they summon analogies as various as a movie, a photo album, the experience of being in an exhibition, a DJ's set, a telephone directory, even a train journey.

The details—far from being extraneous— are integral to whatever COMA designs. All their decisions relating to choice of typeface, stock, orientation of grid, and so on, come directly from whatever concept and organizational structure they've chosen.

COMA's deep understanding of and desire to push each and every one of the conventions of printing is due to their Dutch roots. "In the US, printers tend to be working for clients instead of for designers. In the Netherlands, printers take design very seriously," they say. According to COMA, this is a legacy from a time when printers were publishers, too. Such a rich heritage of bookmaking confers a certain responsibility on today's Dutch book designers. Another difference they've observed is that in the US, production tends to be very separate from design, while in the Netherlands, "A designer does it all." COMA considers that knowledge of formats, bindings, and paper stocks is an essential part of being a good designer.

Such determination and single-mindedness might give the impression that there's little room for other voices—such as the audience's. On the contrary, they say; the audience comes with the content. That's why it's so important to understand this content—it determines its own public. They don't put much store in more conventional methods of audience evaluation such as market research: "If you ask a marketing person what they want, they'll describe something that's already been done—something that's in their visual memory." Graphic design's role, on the other hand, is to find different ways to reformulate the parameters of a problem and to invent a language that's new and previously unimagined. "Our job," say COMA, "is to expand the collective visual memory."

Freezer:
Ice cubes, Nori, Panko,
Cooked Rice, Green Peas,
Bagels

Main Part:
Mustard, Mayo, Honey,
Half and Half, Joghurt,
Butter, Jam Sauce,
Tortillias, Grugere Cheese,
Beer (sixpack)

Beverages:
Seltzer, Grapefruit Juice,
Tomato Juice, Wine Bottle

Lots of veggie "meat"
products (yuck. mostly
unopened). 6 different
kinds of cheese. 2 varieties
of pickles. Decomposing
vegetables. 3 salad
dressings (mostly full).
Mayonnaise (almost gone).
Stacks of take-out/delivery
menus on top (well-worn).

My refrigerator is a small and rectangular in my very small ship's kitchen. It sits quietly on a green marbled linoleum floor. Inside the freezer there is ice and frozen butter, this area often frosts over and I have to use large knives and hot water to break the ice. Below this area is the food. There is a container of Moroccan olives with garlic, a pound of Lily ground coffee, cut up watermelon with mint, a jar of Dijon mustard, a clear container with a cobalt blue lid filled with water, a quart of 2% milk, a lemon, a lime, aloe vera juice and oat nip.

My refrigerator is
white, old (but not
fashionably old) and
sits on a raw 2x4
plinth I built for it so
I don't have to bend
down quite as much.
It's empty except for
beer, wine, milk and
water.
I am not proud of it.

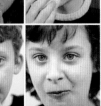

Bellmade sliced roasted eggplants in olive oil, small glass of green pepper, bottle of fresh bio milk, fresh bio butter, cup with sour dough to prepare bread, small package sliced parma ham, parmesan cheese - different types, buffalo milk mozzarella, fresh bio eggs, fresh red onions, lettuce - different sort, capers under salt, spring potatoes, apricot marmelade, fresh zucchini green (sometimes yellow depending if I can find them on the market), french beans, strawberry,

Frame magazine

COMA has art directed this interiors magazine for three years. When they were hired, they decided to change the design with every issue. They wanted to give visual coherence to the issue as a whole rather than to individual articles, as most magazines do. Certain things stay the same across issues, such as the tagline and the body text, but all the other elements—headings, typefaces, the grid and so on—change each time. As soon as they receive the new material for an issue, COMA look for a clue that will lead the design.

Images are kept as big as possible because this has been identified as a factor that helps the magazine to sell well in Asia. It's an international magazine—featuring global interior architecture and design—but, as COMA points out, in many ways it is unmistakably Dutch. There are no adverts within features, and no inserts—advertisers are only offered full pages, and you don't have to flip to the back of the magazine to finish an article. These strategies—all instigated at COMA's insistence—sound simple but would be unheard of in most other magazines. And yet such decisions, far from compromising the magazine's economic viability, have actually led to a doubling of the print run (from 15,000 to 30,000), an increase in the number of pages (from 160 to 192) and more adverts per issue (38 to 53). The magazine's design—which in its flux and constant evolution is a celebration of process and experimentation—reflects the concerns of its audience who are a group of highly trained visual people, and also helps to build that audience. "It's an ongoing search for the perfect shape, the ideal form," say COMA. "Readers and audiences witness this search, experiencing the magazine as design-in-progress, always in flux."

Earthbound on Park Avenue

A restaurant in the lovingly restored Lever House in New York City is the place to go for the ultimate Marc Newson experience.

***Rhythm Science: Paul D. Miller aka DJ Spooky that Subliminal Kid* book**

This small book is part of a series of media pamphlets published by MIT press. In each case, the designer and the author are given equal billing and the opportunity to work together to produce a new kind of book in which the design is far from being an afterthought. The book is in its third printing and has been the most successful in the series so far. "This project was a lesson in the art of the DJ and the art of translation," says COMA of the experience. "A DJ takes one thing—say rhythm or words—and transforms it into something entirely new. And so the approach to this book was to work with the images, ideas, and music that Paul [Miller] gave us—and to deliver something as much brand new as assembled, as much 'us' as him."

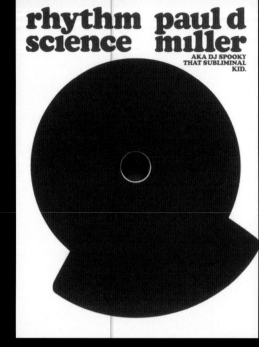

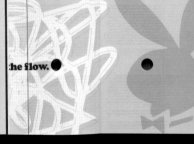

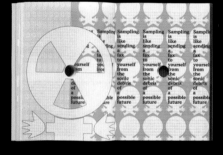

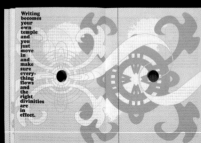

Hella Jongerius

Hella At least your colleagues give you flowers when you have something to celebrate. That never happens if you're a designer. Who'd want to ruin a perfectly good vase by putting flowers in it?

PHAIDON

Louise Then you're talking about art.

Hella No, I'm not talking about art. Useful objects have a rich history. They are saturated with references to specific contexts and specific moments in history. If you refer to that history explicitly and include all the associations in a new story, then you are communicating something, and it's something about useful objects.

Louise So the ideas more or less force you to reduce the functionality?

Hella Er, it's a way of saying something about customs of eating and decorating, about being trapped in conventions and etiquette.

Louise Isn't that rather a lazy way of making exhibitions? You put old and new together, you do a bit of styling…and there you are.

Hella It's not lazy if you're careful to avoid arbitrary combinations. The relations you define say something, and that new story has to be an interesting one. Besides, a new design idea sometimes arises from a job like that, and that is still my main thing, of course, designing.

Hella Jongerius book

COMA describe their design for this book about the Dutch product designer as being "like a train journey." The main text is in the form of an extended conversation between Jongerius and the writer Louise Schouwenberg, and the first question begins on the front cover. COMA gave the interview text and the images their own grids. The text grows up from the base of the page, while the images provide a continuous, horizontally oriented panorama. The bleed means this journey of images through the landscape of the designer's products continues even on the edge of the book. An essay is inserted on vellum to minimize any interruption to the flow: "It's like a trip to the cafeteria on the train," says Hermans. "The journey carries on even while you are reading it."

The quality of the photographs of objects in many countries and contexts was varied so a lot of the work went into finding ones that could be juxtaposed as part of this panorama but still match up in terms of their colors. They printed out all the images and glued them into one long strip, realizing as they did so, how similar this process was to splicing them together like an editor of film. Because Jongerius is interested in the idea of mistakes and imperfection, COMA chose to introduce their own imperfections. Sometimes, for example, the text runs over the images, but they used metallic bronze ink so you can still read it by tipping the book into the light. The monograph speaks to audiences about design and the creative process. As Jongerius points out, the book contains all the stories behind the products, and all the worlds in which the products live.

Good morning, it's January and it's 4:17 a.m., and I'm going to sit here in the dark. I'm in the living room in my blue bathrobe, with an armchair pulled up to the fireplace. There isn't much in the way of open flame at the moment because the underlayer of balled-up newspaper and paper-towel tubes has burned down and the wood hasn't fully caught yet. So what I'm looking at is an orangey ember-cavern that resembles a monster's sloppy mouth, filled with half-chewed, glowing bits of fire-meat. When it's very dark like this you lose your sense of scale. Sometimes I think I'm steering a spaceplane into a gigantic fissure in a dark and remote planet. The planet's crust is beginning to break up, allowing an underground sea of lava to ooze out. Continents are tipping and foundering like melting icebergs, and I must fly in on my highly maneuverable rocket and save the colonists who are trapped there.

AIGA — American Institute of Graphic Arts — It's 4:17 a.m. — 365: AIGA Year in Design 24

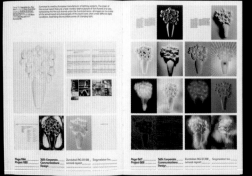

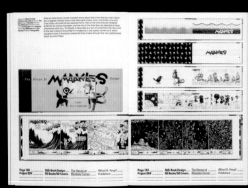

Describe Something Sweet
Box with 120 individually wrapped sugar cubes. COMA asked people of varying ages, professions, and countries to "describe something sweet." Each answer, each story, is told by a sugar cube encased with a wrapper; the handwriting belongs to respondents themselves. "No single response says more than another," say COMA, "And taken together, the answers are revealing: there's silliness, openness, romance, and lust; hunger and loyalty—an infinite universe."

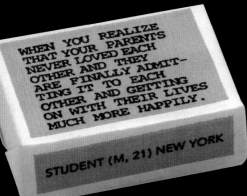

WHEN YOU REALIZE THAT YOUR PARENTS NEVER LOVED EACH OTHER AND THEY ARE FINALLY ADMITTING IT TO EACH OTHER AND GETTING ON WITH THEIR LIVES MUCH MORE HAPPILY.

STUDENT (M, 21) NEW YORK

Light Fluffy. Fuzzy.

STUDENT (M, 24) ?

deValence

On a Thursday evening every two months a standing-room-only crowd of designers gathers at the Palais de Tokyo, one of the hippest cultural venues in Paris, for a design lecture. The organizers of this series manage to engage whichever designer or studio is at the pinnacle of the graphic design zeitgeist at that precise moment—whether it's Stefan Sagmeister, Norm, Optimo, Rik Bas Backer, H5, or Jonathan Barnbrook. The promotional postcards and e-mails are beautifully conceived and produced, and the auditorium is packed every time. It comes as quite a surprise, therefore, to discover that the organizing body behind these events is not a professional design organization, but a loose collective of five friends in their late twenties that go by the name F7. Two of the members, Alexandre Dimos and Gaël Étienne, run the design studio deValence, which serves as the headquarters for F7. The work that Dimos and Étienne do for F7 is characteristic of their other projects, in that it is creative work made for a creative audience.

Dimos and Étienne met one another while studying graphic design at Valence Art School and, in 2001, they joined forces. As deValence, they've already amassed an impressive and interconnected web of clients from the cultural sphere, including art galleries and institutions such as Le Centre Pompidou and Le Palais de Tokyo, and artists like Agnès Thurnauer and Matthieu Laurette. They art direct a music magazine called *Magic* and an art journal called *Le Journal des Laboratoires*. They teach a visual communication class at Marne-La-Vallée and conduct workshops for Bordeaux Art School and Valence Art School. Dimos and Étienne

are best known, however, as the designers-in-residence at Mains d'Œuvres, a cultural center for musicians, painters, dancers, and theater companies, housed in an old warehouse in Saint-Ouen, an industrial suburb to the north of Paris. deValence designed the center's identity and signage using a custom-made font, and continue to produce its regularly appearing posters and flyers.

"Graphic designers have to answer a question asked by people who want to communicate something," say the designers when asked what they think design is for. On a personal level, it's even simpler: "Graphic design is what we do to live," they say.

Eschewing anything to do with what they call "graphic style," deValence is much more interested in identifying the specific qualities of each project and letting these lead their solution. It's very important for them to collaborate meaningfully with the client in each case, as it is he or she that defines most of these specific qualities. "We try to live some good stories with our clients," they say. "We try to understand why the client needs the object he asks for. We try to find out what we could do for him, we try to do it the best we can, and we ask him for help with that. We need him as much as he needs us."

Magic, Revue Pop Moderne magazine covers

Magic, Revue Pop Moderne is a monthly magazine about pop, electronic, and rock music. Clockwise: Cover of 2003 edition with photography by Alexandre Dimos; cover of 2004 edition with illustration by Gaël Étienne; cover of 2005 edition with new logotype design and title font by deValence.

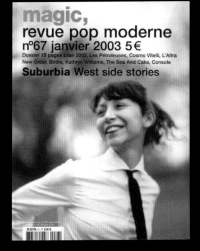

Magic, Revue Pop Moderne spreads

These spreads show the new layout deValence designed in March 2005. It is more dynamic and the title font changes on every issue.

mains d'œuvres

septembre-octobre 2003

18 SEPTEMBRE • PORTES OUVERTES
MAINS D'ŒUV
OUVRE SES PO
+ SOIRÉE DJ'S

20 SEPTEMBRE • CONCERT
ARCHIE BRONS
OUTFIT
+ PANICO

22 SEPTEMBRE • CONCERT
HOMELIFE
+ CINÉMIX

25 ET 26 SEPTEMBRE, 2 ET 3 OCTOBRE • T
« TOKYO < LINE
DE VÉRONIQUE CAYE
dans le cadre de On Life! pour Villet

25 ET 26 SEPTEMBRE, 2 ET 3 OCTOBRE • C
« SORTIR LE DR
EN HIBERNATIO
DE KEITY ANJOURE
dans le cadre de On Life! pour Villet

26 ET 26 SEPTEMBRE, 2 ET 3 OCTOBRE • T
« KAPITAL »
PAR LA KTHA COMPAGNI
dans le cadre de On Life! pour Villet
+ DATES SUPPLEMENTAIRES (LES 28, 29 ET
1ᵉʳ, 9 ET 10 OCTOBRE

25 ET 26 SEPTEMBRE, 2 ET 3 OCTOBRE • VI
PERFORMANCE
« GRENZE »
DE PATRICK FONTANA, AN
ET PIERRE-YVES FAVE
dans le cadre de On Life! pour Villet

MAINS D'ŒUVRES • 1 RUE CHARLES C
HORAIRES, TARIFS, INFOS SUR HTTP:

DIMANCHE 2 NOVEMBRE 2003
CONCERT / 19H30, 8 €

Piano Magic
(4AD/UK)

Margo
(FRANCE)

DJ Laudanum
(FRANCE)

location Fnac, France Billet...

MAINS D'ŒUVRES
1 rue Charles Garnier, 93 400 Saint-Ouen
01 41 11 25 25 www.mainsdoeuvres.org info@mainsdoeuvres.org
metro ligne 13 Garibaldi ou ligne 4 Porte de Clignancourt

MARDI 25 NOVEMBRE 2003
CONCERT / 20H30, 10 €

Him
(FAT CAT/USA)

Gangpol
(FRANCE)

location Fnac, France Billet...

MAINS D'ŒUVRES
1 rue Charles Garnier, 93 400 Saint-Ouen
01 41 11 25 25 www.mainsdoeuvres.org info@mainsdoeuvres.org
metro ligne 13 Garibaldi ou ligne 4 Porte de Clignancourt

MAINS D'ŒUVRES
SEPTEMBRE → OCTOBRE 2004

N
D
2

Left: Mains d'Œuvres event flyers folded and unfolded (below)

Since 2002, deValence have created posters and flyers for the concerts, plays, festivals, exhibitions, dance performances, and conferences that take place at the Mains d'Œuvres cultural center. The relationship began when deValence were looking for a studio: "When we called Mains d'Œuvres, they had no identity and no graphic designers, so we began to collaborate. We rent a low price studio… and we design posters and flyers at low prices, too." They describe the signage they designed for the building as "cheap and efficient." They created a stencil font (Manuel) and printed it using their own laser printer on A4 green fluorescent sheets.

The posters are printed in editions of 5,000. The primary audience for the posters is the population of Saint-Ouen, but they are also distributed to cultural institutions, bars, and clubs throughout Paris. Interestingly, the images on the flyers do not depict the featured artist or performance. deValence wanted to focus more on the lives of the people who look at the flyers—the potential audiences of the events. So they made an illustrated document of contemporary domestic activities such as ironing, locking up a bike, making a call on a cell phone, and so on. "Everybody can recognize himself in the attitudes," say the designers. It was also important to them to find a way for Mains d'Œuvres to "communicate with one voice." Instead of giving every event a different identity, they wanted to show that: "Mains d'Œuvres is talking." They took photos of the various activities, and illustrator Audrey Rasper, made the drawings. At first, it was hard for the designers to persuade their client of the validity of their approach. The music director, for example, wanted the musicians represented on the flyers. He eventually agreed with their direction. When you unfold the flyers and place them next to one another, you notice that the illustrations link from one to the next like an ongoing narrative. "As we knew we had five posters a year to play with, we thought we could, for once, tell a story. We hope we don't just put some letters on some paper. We try to say somethi with what we do. But we do have a 'special message' to say in general about graphic design. Sometimes, a good typeface, well done and composed, is enough." The budget for this project is "… low. Instead of printing some cheap CMYK stuff on some brilliant, coated paper, we decided to print with two beautiful tones on cheap, uncoated paper. People who read the programs are not ve coated themselves. So it is kind of appropriate."

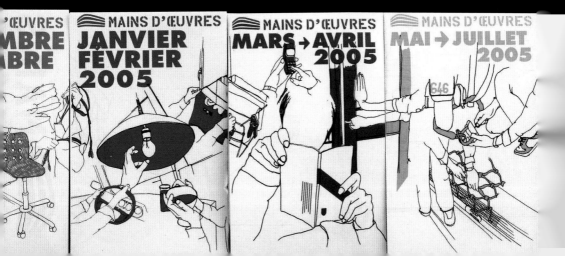

Above: *Le Journal Des Laboratoires*, issue one cover and spreads and *Le Journal Des Laboratoires*, issue two cover and spreads (right)

Le Journal Des Laboratoires is a free booklet published in an edition of 5,000 every six months by the art center Les Laboratoires d'Aubervilliers, and distributed in arts schools, art centers, and galleries. Just like the artists who use the center for their own experimentation, deValence use the *Journal* as a playground for their design. Each issue is designed in a different way. The grid, fonts, paper, the size, and the number of pages change for each issue. The only thing that remains the same is a strip on the cover bearing the title. deValence try to bring experimentation to every project. "We do not have one type of work to make money and one type of work to try things. We try to link both."

SANDY AMERIO / GUILLAUME BAUDIN / MARC BEMBEKOFF
JEAN-MARC CHAPOULIE / YVANE CHAPUIS / CHRISTOPHE FIAT / MARIE GABREAU
AURÉLIEN MOLE / ALEXANDRE NEVEU / JULIE PAGNIER / JAN PETERS / JEAN PODEROS
YVES-NOËL GENOD / QUITERIE GUÉNIOT / RACHEL HAIDU / JOHN MENICK
CÉLINE POULIN
TIPHAINE SAMOYAULT

NUMÉRO TROIS LE JOURNAL DES LABORATOIRES

Above: *Le Journal Des
Laboratoires, issue three
cover and spreads and
Le Journal Des
Laboratoires, issue four
cover and spreads*

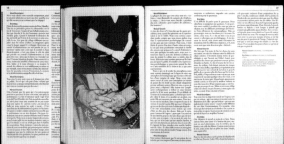

Below: "Art Grandeur Nature" exhibition catalog cover and spreads
Commissioned by Synesthésie and Conseil Général de la Seine-Saint-Denis. The three different fonts used on the cover and in the titles are designed by deValence. Rather than produce what they call a "generic image" for the show, deValence decided instead to list on the cover all the people and partners participating in the exhibition. To give a structure to the book they put text on yellow paper and works on white paper.

Right: Robert Malaval book cover
Published to accompany the solo exhibition of Robert Malaval, held at the Palais de Tokyo in Paris and the eighth Biennial of Contemporary Art of Lyon. "We are bored by paintings on the covers of books about painters," say deValence. And because Robert Malaval is a not very well known but, in the designers' opinion, an important French artist of the last century, they wanted to present him to the reader; "to show how he was looking." So they selected photographs that show some aspects of his life, that they think are as "unbelievable as his work."

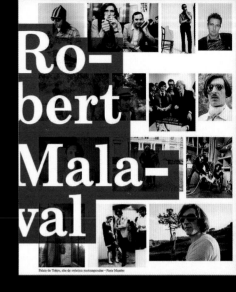

Palais de Tokyo, site de création contemporaine • Paris Musées

Above: Agnes Thurnauer
exhibition catalog

Below: Guillaume Paris
exhibition catalogs

Martin Woodtli

Zürich-based Martin Woodtli is already a notable presence, both in Swiss design and beyond. He is the youngest person to have been invited to join the Alliance Graphique Internationale, winner of the Swiss Federal Design Prize, a feted participant in the European poster festival circuit, and a favorite protégé of Stefan Sagmeister. Despite all the attention, however, this designer is just as interested in what happens when members of the general public encounter his posters as he is by the praise of his peers. "They [the public] say 'that is too complicated for me!' or 'the writing is too small,' 'It looks fresh' or 'it seems dead,'" says Woodtli of his non-designer audience. His work is always created with its social context in mind, and he seems to relish the fact that this place is "not controllable—it is real."

When Woodtli considers a piece of graphic design, he is most interested in how much it "speaks" to him. Only after this assessment does he look to see if it's technically well made or not. As it happens, he is also very exacting when it comes to production. He uses techniques such as silkscreen in a very precise way and is interested in pushing the capabilities of print wherever he can.

Woodtli studied graphic design at the School of Design in Berne, and then at the Zürich Academy of Art and Design. Before setting up his own studio in Zürich, he interned with Sagmeister in New York, who has said of Woodtli's working process: "He is the only person I know who can actually think with the keyboard. His proficiency in various programs is such that he sketches with the keyboard as quickly and uninhibitedly as with pencil and paper."

While Woodtli's graphic language may derive, in large part, from the computer, it is utterly distinct from graphic design's previous attempts to represent the concept of technology, or indeed the profession's fascination with it. Woodtli's work reflects a much more direct engagement with the process of making in the digital medium. His posters are dense, lushly hued, and sculptural. They use complex constructions of typographic and iconographic elements, combined with traces of the way in which they were assembled, to make what appear to be 3D explorations of the 2D poster canvas.

Woodtli spends a lot of time at the beginning of projects determining if he and the client are going to be compatible or not. "The relationship between client and designer is about a balance of power," says Woodtli. "A balance between being open and listening to what people are asking of you and having a clear idea of your own objectives. With some people you can have an informal relationship and it still works. With others you must define yourself more strongly. For the sake of you and your client, it is important to create a relationship that permits you to do your job as well as possible."

He continues: "If you do something with all your heart and intelligence and you know why you do it, then, in some circumstances, it can have a better result than working for the sake of it." Woodtli does not believe in such things as a stroke of genius or that design could be, "Something you do on the side." He says, "Design, for me, is about having lots of energy, and, in the best case, an obsession where you act on your own interests and goals."

19. JUNI BIS
22. AUGUST
2004

lichtecht

GESTALTUNG
ZUERICH

...STELLUNGSSTRASSE 60
...ER CH

OEFFNUNGSZEITEN:
...-SO 10-20 UHR / FR-SO 11-18 UHR

objekt
licht
wirkung

Left: "VideoEx" poster
Silkscreen poster for "VideoEx," an experimental movie and video festival.

Right: "Play" exhibition poster
Commissioned by the Museum Für Gestaltung, Zürich. This exhibition examined the theme of play through the forms that it generates. It included known works such as Monopoly and Die Siedler Von Catan, as well as unknown things, like games in the future. Geared towards a design-savvy audience, the show explored the psychology of play as well as the designed objects associated with it.

Below: "Door 2 Door" poster
This poster was designed to promote a three-day festival that took place in Berne, Switzerland, featuring the work of 90 artists, an international symposium, and various exhibitions in all of Berne's artistic institutions.

Right: "Sportdesign" exhibition poster
Commissioned by the Museum Für Gestaltung Zürich. The premise of this exhibition was that design for sports falls somewhere between style and engineering and infiltrates our lives through the appliances, clothing, and communications that we use every day.

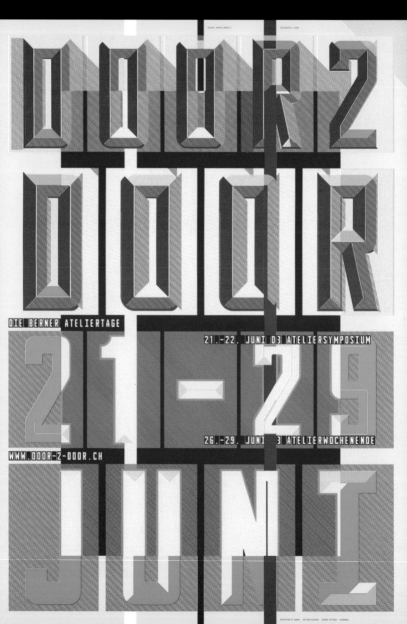

MUSEUM FüR GESTALTUNG ZüRICH

SPORT DESIGN

13. NOVEMBER 2004–13. MäRZ 2005

DI–DO 10–20h / FR–SO 11–18h / 24.12., 31.12., 11–16h / MONTAGS SOWIE 25.12., 1.1. GESCHLOSSEN / AUSSTELLUNGSSTRASSE 60, 8005 ZÜRICH

Clarissa Tossin

"Brazil is definitely part of my work and it always flavors my approach to design," says Clarissa Tossin, a designer and illustrator who lives and works in São Paulo, Brazil. "It is one among many aspects of my daily life that influence and inspire me."

Tossin enjoys a fluid and interdependent relationship with her collaborators and clients, both local and international. As such, her studio, A', is typical of a new kind of flexible hybrid design practice that is able to expand and contract in response to the needs of various commissions, involving various media, in different parts of the world. Her regular collaborators include musicians such as Bizarre Music, programmers and designers like Dimitre Lima, fashion designers such as Karlla Girotto, and artists. Her clients are *Vogue Brasil*, MTV Brasil, MTV Latina, Trama Records, São Paulo Fashion Week, Liquid Frontiers (Austria), O2 Filmes, Gullane Filmes, and Galeria Vermelho.

In Tossin's experience, MTV, whether in the US or Brazil, is a very open-minded client. "Everything goes," she says. "They give us designers plenty of freedom to come up with something fresh." The MTV Quickie (US) is an animated abstraction with what Tossin calls "the light and shiny spirit of Sundays." For MTV Brazil, she was more specific and used the visual metaphors of cross section, sea level, and rising temperature to express the program's subject matter. At that time in her personal work, Tossin was already formally investigating textures and layers, and developing her typeface, Irvore. With this promo, she found a commercial space in which she could continue these investigations.

"Usually, the information I get about the audience is very superficial and generic," says Tossin. So the starting point for the "creation process" comes from the client's message and knowing what the piece will be used for, what its context will be. "Graphic design, at least from a market perspective, is for communicating more efficiently, selling ideas and products, making things look better," Tossin concludes. On a personal level, graphic design is simply "the creative field" she gravitates toward for self-expression and to explore her skills.

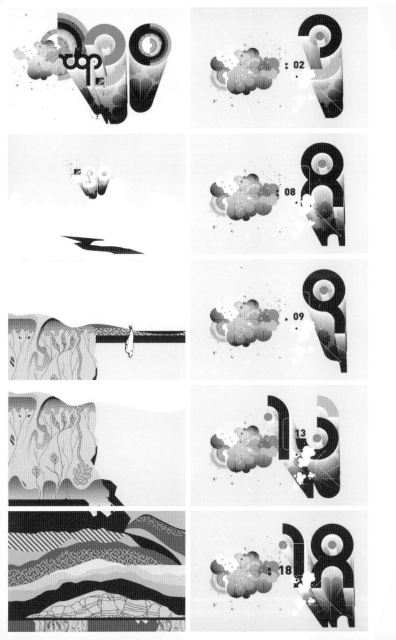

Urban Wallpaper Mural

Lambe-lambe is a type of poster native to Brazil that is printed cheaply in one or two primary or fluorescent colors, on thin paper stock. Its literal translation from the Portuguese is "licking-licking," which refers specifically to the way in which the posters are applied to walls—with paste and big brushes in a "licking" motion. The low cost of its production makes lambe-lambe a popular choice for the promotion of shows and cultural events. Tossin was asked to create a poster that would be showcased for the duration of digital film festival, Resfest Brazil, on the walls of the São Paulo Museum Of Art metro station's exit corridors. Her solution was to use the lambe-lambe technique. The budget was very low to start with and, because Tossin's design needed to be printed across three sheets, she had to cut costs even further.

One decided to use just black because it was "basic," and because "I wanted people to be able to read the text—the introductory paragraph of the book *Passion According to G.H.* by Clarice Lispector (1988)." Tossin relished the inherent limitations of this process and made a point of incorporating them in the design. "Ultimately, this became a very personal piece," she says. Only enough posters were printed to cover the metro station's exit corridors. But Tossin printed some more at about a third of the original size to sell at an A' Yard Sale, an on-line bric-a-brac store that supports her personal production.

Right: CD cover for the 5th São Paulo Fashion Week CD compilation

The brief from the client was to find inspiration in the object known as "Giramundo;" a toy made in northeastern Brazil from colorful fabric laces that rotates according to the wind, often used during carnival parties.

Far Right: CD cover for the 6th São Paulo Fashion Week CD compilation:

The theme for the event was the melting pot of the Brazilian population and the colorful variety in skin colors its miscegenation has created.

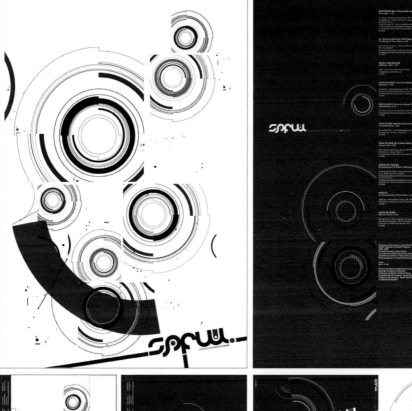

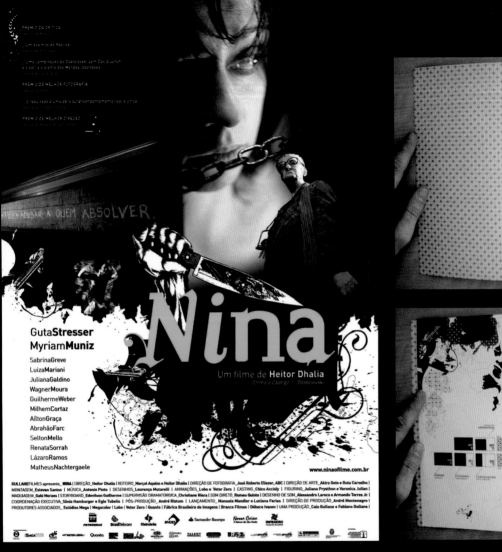

Above: Nina visual identity

Tossin created a visual identity for the Brazilian movie *Nina*. The identity was used on a range of promotional materials. The movie is about a young girl, Nina, who is tormented by various theories and anxieties, struggling to live on her own as if she were in someone else's body." The fact that Nina is an illustrator provided Tossin with a rich theme to use in her design. The catalog was used as a promotional piece. It was distributed in international festivals as a souvenir after special screenings, and also

Right: MTV "Quickie" promo
This eight-second promo was
designed for *Sunday Stew*,
a medley of MTV programs,
including *Wildboyz* and *Viva
La Bam*. Tossin recalls the
brief as being "Anything.
Everything." US-based motion
graphics company, Brand
New School, commissioned
Tossin and animated her
illustrations and storyboards.
"My task was to catch the
attention of the audience, and
make them want to watch the
program," she says.

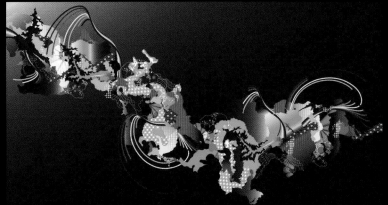

Radovan Jenko

Radovan Jenko works in a big 100-year-old building in Ljubljana, the capital of Slovenia. With a population of only 300,000, Ljubljana is a small city with an old quarter through which flows the river Ljubljanica. Two hours from Venice and four hours from Vienna, with: "Charming places where you can take a glass of good wine and have a chat with friends." Ljubljana is, according to poster artist and designer Jenko, "A good environment for imagination and creativity."

Jenko studied poster art with Professor Henryk Tomaszewski and painting with Professor Teresa Pagowska in the late 1970s at the Academy of Fine Arts in Warsaw. Today, Radovan Jenko is a Professor at Ljubljana University, Academy of Fine Arts and Design, and runs a studio where he designs posters, calendars, books, and illustrative logos. His clients are primarily cultural institutions such as museums and publishers, but he also works for a bank and for friends.

Even though his clients are all from Ljubljana and Celje, Jenko's influence extends well beyond this close-knit community. He regularly serves as a juror for international poster competitions, receives awards from as far afield as the Internet Design Competition in Tokyo, ZGRAF in Zagreb, and the Art Directors Club in New York. His posters are in the permanent collections of the Israel Museum in Jerusalem, Die Neue Sammlung in Munich, and the Dansk Plakatmuseum in Aarhus, Denmark.

Jenko sees himself as an interpreter, working at: "A crossroads where translation between the verbal and the visual takes place." The visual language of his posters is rich, both in dense, illustrative, and typographic detail, and in resonant metaphoric content. Like distilled visual poems, his posters use wit, a contemporary take on visual surrealism, and an assortment of playful flourishes such as handwritten text and layers of imagery that only emerge when you look closely, to captivate the viewer and to deliver often hard-hitting messages. His posters address subjects as various as an upcoming play in Dubrovnik, global consumerism, and ecological sustainability. At the same time as wanting to surprise the viewer with his unique brand of visual thinking, Jenko says he also wants his work to be: "Simple and understandable to its audiences. I want to achieve a perfect synergy of information, image, design, and parties."

"To me, it's always important to know who my audience is," says Jenko. As soon as he has this information, he prefers to make his own comment on the subject at hand. "This way I can take more surprising turns," he says.

According to Jenko, "Graphic design is for communication—powerful communication." On a personal level, it's also about: "Working hard and having fun at the same time, and then maybe, just maybe, the magic of art occurs every now and then."

"Deadly Funny" poster
The starting point for this poster, intended to promote a satirical cabaret, was the picture of the show's performer Andrej Rozman-Roza. Jenko used handwritten typography as a response to the improvisational nature of Roza's performance. 1,000 posters were printed and displayed throughout Slovenia, mostly in Ljubljana. The text translates as: Deadly Funny; Andrej Rozman-Roza and his cultural twist present Cabaret Simplosion with a selection of evening songs; commercial interruptions; live music!

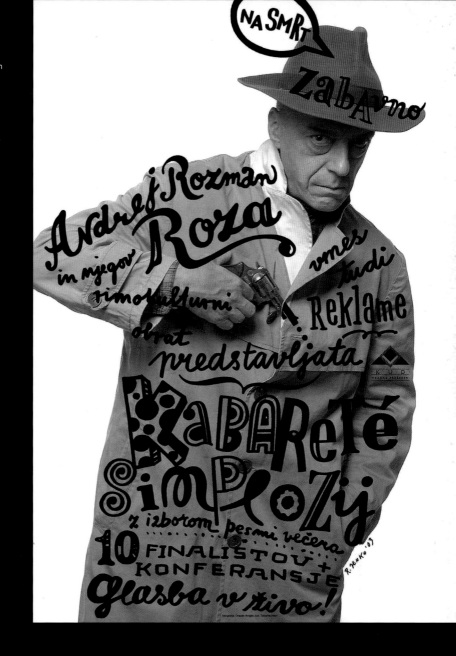

Left: Calendar illustration
A page from a self-promotional
calendar called "2000—The
Great Leap Year."

With this illustration, Jenko
wanted to portray death as
"something nice," rather than
"the end of everything." He
depicted a skull in the shape of
a heart and incorporated in the
illustration "friendly flowers."

Left: Le Petit poster

When asked by Prizmic & Brill Valise et Compagne Inc. to create a poster for a theater festival in Dubrovnik, Jenko considered the following factors and combined them to make the poster's evocative image: "The client's love of angels and beautiful women, the atmosphere of the festival, and the ever-charming city of Dubrovnik."

Right: The Woman And The Sea

This was used to illustrate a story about the author's experience when she went sailing with her husband and their children.

Above: ***By The River Piedra I Sat Down and Wept*** **poster**

This silkscreen poster was produced in an edition of 500 for Vale Novak Publishing to promote a new book by Paulo Coelho, titled *By The River Piedra I Sat Down and Wept* landscape to symbolize the structure of the book's love story, and within it he "hid" the sitting girl as a metaphor for what he calls: "The power of love leading through transformation, and the female divine principle."

barbara says

"Graphic design can be seen as a way of embodying and pointing out the complexities and intricacies of everyday life," says António Silveira Gomes, whose design collective, barbara says, is located in Lisbon. Such a view runs counter to a more traditional notion of graphic design as an agent of clarity. That's because barbara says—a constantly mutating group of designers dedicated to: "Stimulating a fuller comprehension of lowbrow culture, and to hastening its absorption by the mainstream establishment"—is not a traditional design firm. The collective originally had five members, who met in the late 1990s while studying on the Communication Design Course at Faculdade de Belas Artes at the University Of Lisbon. Today, the group's most consistent presence is Silveira Gomes and his most regular collaborators are José Albergaria and Nuno Horta Santos.

"Culturally, we [Portugese] are very nostalgic and contemplative," says Silveira Gomes. As an example of the way in which these cultural roots feed his work, he points to a catalog he designed for an art exhibition, "The Name Written on Your Bosom", the theme of which was a famous Portuguese medieval love tragedy, deeply rooted, as Silveira Gomes puts it, "In our melancholic-romantic tradition." Silveira Gomes is regularly drawn to the graphic details of the Portuguese vernacular, and, in this case, it was the patterns used in traditional pastry packaging that informed his design for the catalog. He exploited the contrast between the cheap duplex cardboard used for the pastry boxes with complex hand finishes. He's ambivalent about the success of this piece, however, because, in his opinion, he did not connect as fully as he could with his audience. Some people missed the reference to the pastry and, "Just thought it was retro."

"I believe that knowing about the audience is important to every aspect of a project—its form, its content, and its dissemination," says Silveira Gomes. "Through knowing and understanding the audience, I learn a lot about my work as a graphic designer." He only wishes there were more time to study this process. He'd like to know, for example, when and where the lifecycle of a poster or a Web site begins and ends—if it is understood or not, set aside and forgotten or re-appropriated and recycled. Silveira Gomes is researching this aspect of design—at least in a theoretical sense—as part of his MA studies. His idea is to create a local newspaper for a specific community—the urban zone that comprises two Lisbon quarters, Bairro Alto and Bica. The publication will function as a normal newspaper—bringing information to its audience—and it will also be an interactive platform through which the audience may express their views and opinions. At a third level, the platform becomes a way to observe and study the behavior and culture of the audience and its environment. The title for the publication, *Pão* (bread), emerged from the idea of using available bakeries in the area as the broadcasting centers for the newspaper.

"I wish I could impregnate in everything I design the possibility of getting raw data feedback from the audience," he muses. "It's easier to get spontaneous reactions, however—and, in the end, they are probably more honest."

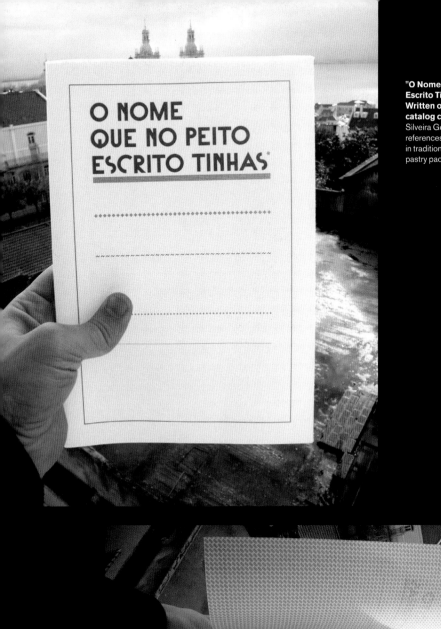

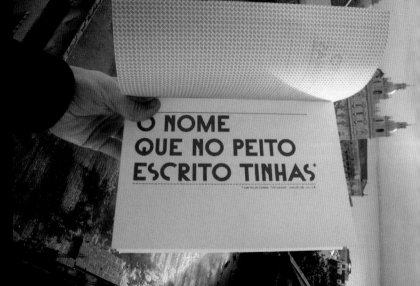

n°3

flirt

grátis

FLIRT

Flirt magazine

Flirt, published by the Galeria
Zé Dos Bois, began as a guide
to the Bairro Alto neighborhood
of Lisbon and grew into a
cultural opinion magazine. The
distribution was very hands-on
and ad hoc. It involved the

designers taking a stack of
magazines and leaving them
at the gallery office every time
they went to see an exhibition,
and Manuel Henriques, one of
the publishers, driving around
to all the museums and galleries
in central Lisbon. *Flirt* lasted
for 27 issues, was distributed
for free, and had articles in
both English and Portuguese.

Formato seminar poster

Designed by António Silveira
Gomes and Mafalda Anjos.
When the Portuguese
Architects Guild, Ordem Dos
Arquitectos, organized a
seminar to review its official
monthly magazine in the
context of other printed
and on-line architecture
publications, it asked barbara
says to create a poster to
promote the event. The
designers looked at a number
of architecture books: "I
purposefully left out Rem
Koolhaas and Bruce Mau's
S, M, L, XL (1997, Monacelli
Press)," says Silveira Gomes.
"I looked for more obscure
publications—there is a
*Lithuanian Association of
Architects* magazine, for
example." Some of the
publications were connected
to event speakers and some
were vintage, in Silveira
Gomes's effort to connect
with older generations of
architects. The organizers of
the event wanted to discuss
issues like transitional media in
publishing and the competition
from independent publishing
especially in digital media, and
Silveira Gomes convinced
them that "Formato," or
"Format" in English, was the
perfect name. "I had been
thinking about lettering built
from objects and, when I saw
José Albergaria and Rik Bas
Backer developing a floppy
disk typeface, I realized what
the title for this seminar should
be; it connected immediately
with the intent of the client's
message." The designers at
barbara says photographed
the books individually, opened
them in Photoshop, and
composed the letterforms
without repeating any covers.

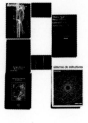

7 > ▓ MAIO 2004

POLÍTICA EDITORIAL
DE ARQUITECTURA

Sede da Ordem dos Arquitectos
Travessa do Carvalho 21-23, 1249-003 LISBOA

DEBATES E MOSTRA
DE PUBLICAÇÕES ESTRANGEIRAS

SEXTA-FEIRA, 7 DE MAIO (Entrada Livre)
••
• 18h00 • Sessão de Abertura
• 19h00 • Inauguração da Mostra
de Publicações Estrangeiras

SÁBADO, 8 DE MAIO (Inscrição Obrigatória)
••
• 10h00 • Sessão 1 – Publicações Periódicas
• 14h30 • Sessão 2 – Edições
• 18h00 • Sessão de Encerramento

Inscrições até 30 de Abril para:
Tel. 21 3241161 • Fax 21 3241170
• E-mail: cultura2@oasrs.org
• Para mais informações: www.oasrs.org
••
Custo de Inscrição €30 • Membros da O.A. €15
• Estudantes €15

Organização: Ordem dos Arquitectos – Secção Regional do Sul

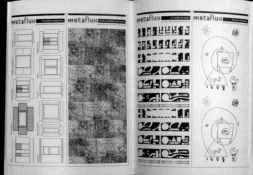

Metaflux catalog and decal brochure

Designed by António Silveira Gomes, Mafalda Anjos, and Francisca Mendonça. Portuguese representation at the 2004 Venice Architecture Biennial consisted of a visual display of the work of ten architects and five artists who work with the themes of architecture and urbanization. barbara says developed an identity system for each architect that included a brochure made of adhesive transparency film that contained observations and more abstract aspects of their work. "The adhesive film brochure was an experimental solution playing with standardization and spontaneous communication systems like stickers and tags," says Silveira Gomes. There was an unexpected level of feedback regarding the adhesive films and Silveira Gomes is, "Still hoping to run into some applications made with such stickers."

APPLICATION FORM   ORIGINAL

TRANSFER
USA / PORTUGAL Immigration Agency
www.zedosbois.org/transfer

START HERE

PERSONAL INFORMATION

Name: _____

Contact: _____

Age: [ ]

Sex: M [ ]   F [ ]   Lucky Number: [ ][ ][ ][ ][ ][ ]

Love Status: In Love [ ]   Not in love [ ]   Broken Hearted [ ]

Current Profession: _____

PSYCHOLOGICAL PROFILE

1. Do you suffer from any physical or mental illnesses?

Yes [ ]   No [ ]

If yes, which? _____

2. Pick three items:

TRANSFER

HELP

3. Mark your expectations for the next 12 months in the TRANSFER scale:

(JUL, AUG, SEP, OCT, NOV, DEZ, JAN, FEV, MAR, APR, MAY, JUN — 2001-2002)

4. Which have you done inside a museum?

Scream [ ]   Fill a form [ ]   Obscene drawings in the W.C. [ ]

Shoplift from the gift shop [ ]   Touch an artwork [ ]

TRANSFER USE ONLY

KEEP THE COPY
PLACE THE ORIGINAL IN THE BOX OR SEND IT BY POST MAIL TO:
ZDB GALLERY, R. DA BARROCA, 59, 1200-047 LISBOA, PORTUGAL

11. Why do you want to leave your country?

Other [ ]
Patriotism [ ]   Nature [ ]   Self [ ]
Ownership [ ]   Community [ ]   WWW [ ]
Family [ ]   Market [ ]   Religion [ ]

10. Number these items in a scale from 1 to 10:

(Select one item and write an appropriate question for your answer)

9. _____

8. Any prior cases of emigration in your family history?

Yes [ ]   No [ ]

If yes, state the last 3 cases:

7. Which of these maps corresponds to Portugal?

6. When standing in line your patience runs out after:

1 min. [ ]   5 min. [ ]   20 min. [ ]   1 hour [ ]

5. Create your ideal daily schedule:

HELP

IMMIGRANT PROFILE

RƎꟻꙄИAЯT TRANSFER

TRANSFER   TRANSFER   TRANSFER   TRANSFER

↰ Insert original here   ↰ Insert original here
and keep the copy   and keep the copy

"Transfer" exhibition
Designed by António Silveira
Gomes, Nuno Horta Santos of
Barbara says for a collaborative
exhibition between the ZDB
gallery in Lisbon and the Yerba
Buena Center for the Arts in
San Francisco. ZDB set up a
nonprofit immigration agency
to enable American citizens
to work in Portugal and to
experience its culture.

Base

In 1993 Dimitri Jeurissen, Thierry Brunfaut, and Juliette Cavanaile set up a small graphic design studio in Brussels. Base—a name that refers to a grounded quality of honesty and directness discernible in the firm's work—now has additional offices in Barcelona, Madrid, New York, and Paris.

Base specializes in creative direction and brand development for a broad range of clients. Most of this work stems from direct client commissions, but Base also likes to create as much space as possible for self-initiated projects. BaseWORDS is dedicated to creative writing; BaseMOTION specializes in film and motion graphics, and BaseLAB is where custom typefaces and design tools are built.

Most of these new initiatives are generated by one of the five partners and their personal interests. These interests, as well as the people connected to them, can lead to new locations for studios. "You find people you feel comfortable with and then you start doing things together and it builds up," Jeurissen says. "That's how we ended up with studios in Barcelona and New York." The potential for expansion is not limitless, Jeurissen points out: "I have the impression that once your studios get detached from the core, the firm becomes a brand and evolves into something else. Happily, I don't know what that is yet."

Each Base studio has its own activity based on local markets, in addition to the international clients. "The fashion and branding industry is bigger in New York and we tend to do more books in Brussels," says Jeurissen. "For example, I'll do the creative direction for a Spanish underwear company or the rebranding for a Belgian TV station from New York. I'm taking advantage of this big production platform where you have everybody in the city to do great work."

Jeurissen is interested in the way all the studios interact almost seamlessly: "Something I want to encourage is that, at the end of a job, you don't know who did what, because there's been input from everyone—from the ideas and conceptual stage to development and production."

Base treads a fine line between the global and the local. "What's interesting is living in Brooklyn, and designing a restaurant for someone just down the road, but also going to Barcelona, Paris, London, Madrid, and Brussels, and absorbing all those local influences that will at a certain point pop up in what you're doing," says Jeurissen. What annoys him is the type of shop or hotel that looks the same the world over. "If a client wants to make a global brand and has the power to develop it globally, then that's one strategy, but we always try to find twists that are local within that strategy." For example, Base has developed different campaigns and identities for subdevelopments within the Puma brand, such as Mahanuala and 96 Hours. "[Puma] want to find alternatives to heavy corporate and global branding. They are working more locally," he says.

According to Base partner Geoff Cook, graphic design is about communicating using ideas: "From the phone book to the subway, graphic design enables communication ultimately in an attempt to make the world a better place."

Beople magazine covers and spreads
Flouting accepted rules of editorial design, Base put a white dot over the cover model's head, in part to defy the cover girl formula, but also because Belgium doesn't have any internationally recognized celebrities.

LOUD identity system
LOUD creates and organizes festivals, produces TV shows, programs closed-circuit TV channels, and consults for fashion designers. Base observed how, in its bustling creative office, LOUD would constantly use Post-it notes so they decided to build the identity around this humble stationery item. They used different colored Post-its to identify LOUD's various areas of activity, turning an everyday object into a complete system of identification.

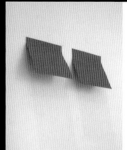

LOUD
POST-IT
SIGNAGE
SYSTEM

LOUD

Passeig de Sant Joan 2/Entl.1/Barcelona 08010/Spain
T+34 932476050/F+34 932476052/loud@loud.es/www.loud.es

☐ Carta   ☐ Fax   ☐ Presupuesto   ☐ Factura nº

"Johnny" campaign

The idea for this enigmatic campaign for a contemporary art exhibition, shows, and events at the Palais Des Beaux-Arts in Brussels was to make people wonder what, or who, Johnny is. Base designed and produced the promotional "speech bubble" stickers for use in a guerrilla-marketing street campaign. Messages were included in some of the bubbles, and others were left empty, enabling the client to create and print any message they wanted. For a reasonably small show this proved a direct, inexpensive, and effective solution.

"Primavera Sound"
festival identity
Base was commissioned
to design a new identity for
Barcelona's annual three-day
music festival, Primavera
Sound, including its Web
site, ad campaign, printed
materials, and tickets.

ENFIN!
AU COEUR DE BRUXELLES!
LE NOUVEAU
THEATRE
NATIONAL
DE LA COMMUNAUTÉ FRANÇAISE
OUVRE SES PORTES AU PUBLIC!
GRAND FESTIVAL
D'OUVERTURE
DU 19 NOVEMBRE AU 6 DECEMBRE
SPECTACLES, MUSIQUE, FÊTE, LUMIÈRE
VIN, AMOUR ET FANTAISIE!
INFORMATIONS ET RESERVATIONS: TÉL.: 02 2035303, EMAIL: LOCATION@THEATRENATIONAL.BE
THEATRE NATIONAL: 111-115 BD EMILE JACQMAIN, 1000 BRUXELLES

Chelsea Carwash

Carwash   Lube   Gaz   Market

ORG

"Consider the design of a ConEd electricity bill," says David Reinfurt, the founder of the ORG design firm in New York. "The bill arrives in the customer's mailbox and it's immediately apparent what to pay, what you bought, and what your average uses over the quarter are. At the same time, the form is so precisely organized, and in bright [ConEd] blue, with bold and crisp bits, that it also gives you the idea that ConEd is a smart, organized, and responsive public utility." The bill, according to Reinfurt is an example of design that: "Transcends its original function while still answering the original brief." And that, he says, is precisely what the best graphic design does.

ORG's clients vary in character from small art galleries, to large universities, to public trusts. The company works in a range of media, including print, environmental, and electronic applications such as Web sites and custom software.

Reinfurt has a strong belief that a design must change, or at least be open to change. He does not separate personal and professional projects and ORG's headquarters hosts a constantly shifting population of designers, each with different areas of expertise who are, as he puts it, "Openly sharing and assimilating ideas into a larger framework."

"Graphic design is for saying a certain thing to a certain group in a certain setting, so nicely that other groups get interested and other meanings arise." This encapsulation of graphic design's purpose—Reinfurt's response to the question "What is graphic design for?"—identifies the motivation behind much of ORG's work.

For Reinfurt, the audience for a graphic design project is essential. In fact, it is often what directly drives his design decisions. He finds it more useful, however, to think in terms of multiple audiences rather than one audience. The latter, he says, "Sounds like a prescriptive 'target demographic,' or some such." Designing for one audience is a problematic concept for Reinfurt because, "It doesn't leave room for the work to respond to change or, "Transcend its original function while still answering the original brief," in the way that the ConEd bill does.

An example of work that "transcends" or, at least, evolves from its original function is found in a construction fence that he has created at the World Trade Center site as part of the StoryCorps oral history project. Here, a pattern emerges over time as commuters pass through the station. Posters become pixels in what Reinfurt refers to as: "The world's slowest and most analog LED display screen." This clearly plays off its context and the presence of its audience as it incorporates into its very fabric the movements of the commuters who pass by every day. So many tourists were taking photographs of it, Reinfurt was told, that the construction workers at the site believe it to be the most documented construction fence on record. "Of course," admits Reinfurt, "The tourists probably assumed it had something more specifically to do with Ground Zero, but it is an interesting result in any case."

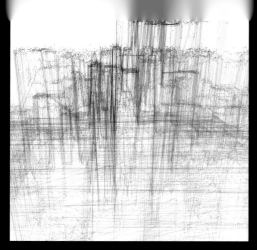

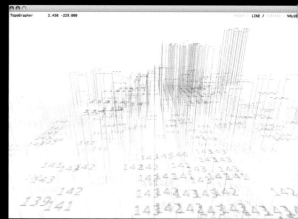

Spatial Information Design Lab at Columbia University School of Architecture software

This is a new collaboration between Reinfurt and the architects Laura Kurgan and Mark Wigley, which uses Geographic Information Systems to track and display criminal justice patterns for a School of Architecture project. "I'm developing some custom graphic software that reads these databases and quickly creates maps on the fly," Reinfurt says. "The hope is that these maps can be used to help shape public governmental policy." The images pictured represent the distribution of parole officers in Wichita, Kansas.

ORG 203

Vernon Boulevard

Queens Plaza Station

Long Is City identity

The goal of this project, which involved an architect, an art historian, and ORG, was to improve the ways that residents and visitors access the nine major arts institutions in Long Island City. After rejecting the possibility of connecting the arts venues through physical means, the group decided instead to create what Reinfurt calls: "An urban graphics strategy," that would link the venues virtually in the visitor's mind. For inspiration, Reinfurt, a resident of Long Island City himself, drew on the resources at hand, which, in this case, were typographic. Reinfurt observed that on the G train, the buses and local postage franks, his neighborhood is referred to by the abbreviation "Long Is City." Reinfurt developed a graphic identity that depicted the phrase "Long Is City" using the visual language of the Pepsi-Cola sign on the Queens bank of New York's East River. The logo, inspired by the red neon cursive insignia was officially adopted by Long Island City Cultural Alliance and has since been used on billboards, T-shirts, a Web site, and a series of quarterly guides that contain a map and listings information.

StoryCorps project

Reinfurt designed all the print and environmental graphic design for StoryCorps, an ongoing project created to: "Record the stories of average Americans." The original audio recording booth is in Grand Central Station, New York. A second booth has opened near the World Trade Center site, and includes the graphics for a construction fence and a sequence of posters for the World Trade Center Path train station. The project will also be touring the country in mobile Airstream trailers. Reinfurt developed a pattern based on silhouetted figures for use on the various applications. The kiosk exterior is a sandwich channel with backlit graphics, causing the figures to shift as you walk around it. At the WTC, the booth is made from Panelite, a glass composite material that veils the view into the booth. The main StoryCorps letters are made from written transcripts of previous StoryCorps interviews.

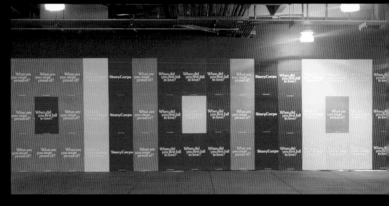

מודעה

שלום במזרח התיכון:
מכתב גלוי של יהודים אמריקאים לממשלתם

שפיכות הדמים בעת האחרונה במזרח התיכון הביאה ישראלים ופלסטינים רבים — ואת תומכיהם בארה"ב — לאורח מחשבה של אתנו-כנגד כאשר כל צד רואים את עצמם כקורבנות צדיקים ומתעלמים או מפמיעים את העוולות שעושי וממשיכים לעשותם לעם האחר.

לאמיתו של דבר שני העמים הישראלי והפלסטיני סבלו עוולות רבות מידי העם השני, גם אם באופנים שונים וללא השוואה: לשנויים תלונות לגיטימיות, פחדים לגיטימיים, וחוסר אמון לגיטימי ברצונו של העם השני להתפשר למען השלום.

להותמי מכתב זה מגוון רחב של דעות על היחסים האחריות למצב שנגרד, אך יש להם השקפה משותפת על המרכיבים הכרחיים של הסכם.

צעדים הדרגתיים לבניית אמון הגיעו למבוי סתום. החלופה היחידה למלחמה ללא סוף היא הסדר כולל המבוסס על עקרונות פשוטים אך מרחיקי לכת:

* חיי ישראלים ופלסטינים שווי ערך.
* לשני העמים, הישראלי והפלסטיני, זכויות שווה להגדרה-עצמית לאומית ולחיים של שלום וביטחון.
* לשני העמים, הישראלי והפלסטיני, זכויות שווה לחלק הוגן של האדמה והמשאבים של פלסטין (ארץ ישראל) ההיסטורית.

צופים הוגנים ברחבי העולם הבינו זה זמן רב ובבהירות את הכרוך בפתרון בר-קיימא, המכובד את העקרונות שלעיל:

* שתי מדינות לאומיות, ישראל ופלסטין, בעלות ריבונות שווה, זכויות שווה וחובות שווה.
* חלוקה לאורד גבולות 67 עם תיקונים שולים מוסכמים.
* פינוי מלא של כל ההתנחלויות בשטחים הכבושים, למעט אלו שבשטחים שיוחלפו.
* הכרה פלסטינית וערבית בישראל תוך על הבטחת טריטוריאלית נוספת.
* קבלה פלסטינית, במשא ומתן, של "זכות שיבה" מוגבלת כנגד פיצוים נספים לפליטים.

לפני שנים אחדות הראו סקרים שרוב הישראלים והפלסטינים היו נכונים לקבל הסדר פשרה מסוג זה. למרות הסבה הנוכחי, יתכן שעדיין אלו פני הדברים; אך הסברה קשה כאשר הרוב בשני הצדדים תומך בפעולות התגרות צבאיות שכל צד מתאר כפעולות הגנה נגד צורפה, בעוד מיעוטים בעלי עוצמה מקדמים מטרות הממשטות מירבית.

אם אין ברצונם אן ביכולתם לנהל משא ומתן לשלום מעשי, חובתה של הקהילה הבינלאומית להנהיג את הקדומו. לא רק למען האינטרס ארוך-הטווח של ישראלים ופלסטינים. אלא גם אלו של אמריקאים: אירוע הזמן האחרון בהכירו באומן מכאיב שביטחוננו הלאומי מאים באופן חמור על ידי חוסר-יציבות ואי-צדק במזרח התיכון.

לארה"ב אחריות מיוחדת למבוי הסתום הטרגי הנוכחי, לנוכח התמיכה הכלכלית והצבאית העצומה שניתנה לממשלת הישראלית 5005 לאזור ישראלי לשנה. לארצנו יש מנוף-תשפע יוצא-דופן. כיהודים אמריקאים שביטחוותה ארוך טוותח של ישראל יקר לליבם, אנו קוראים לממשלתנו להתנות המשך הסיוע הכלכלי בקבלה ישראלית של הסדר שתי-מדינות שיוסבב באופן בינלאומי.

סרבנו שני הצדדים יתקפו זה הסדר מסוג זה. יתכן מאד ויידרשו כוחות זרים לאכיפתו, ועליהם להיות נכונים לסבול אבידות. אך ניתן בכל לקות שהרוב הישראלי כמו גם הפלסטיני יבר בכך שטוב שלום פגום ממלחמה נצחית.

אין כל ערובה שגישה זו תיצלח; אולם ודאי לחלוטין שכל החלופות תיכשלנה.

אנא שלחו תרומה לפ לעזר את המודעי!
לניווח חתימות על זו, או לקבלת מידע נוסף, אנשר לפנות אל:
SOKAL-PHYSICS.NYU.EDU (ALAN SOKAL)
בניין השם של שברולנד ח"ב בקרקו, עאר ת האוני.
אשר גם לכתוב ל-
BRUCE ROBBINS
DEPARTMENT OF ENGLISH AND COMPARATIVE PHILOSOPHY HALL
COLUMBIA UNIVERSITY, NY, NY 10027
תיופות לסיוע מעין מזונו ל-ב בעי מזגו נגברה.
את הרמסאות ׳ש לכתוב ׳ש לשם: PEACE IN THE MIDDLE EAST

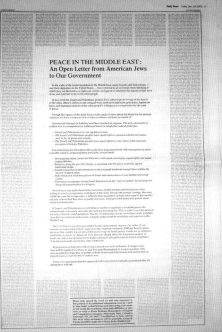

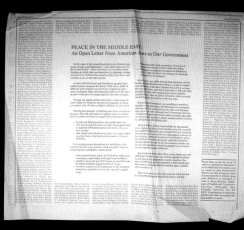

Open Letter generative newspaper advertisement

This project was conceived to serve as a voice for the American Jewish community. The newspaper advertisement is for an advocacy group in New York called Peace in the Middle East. In addition to the letter advocating peace, the text of the advertisement includes the names of the people who have signed on to the cause, along with a request for donations. Everyone who donates is included in subsequent ads.

The first ad ran in the *New York Times*. "It was very successful and the money kept pouring in, allowing it to be rerun in newspapers again and again, all around the country and the world, and reaching a small, but geographically dispersed audience," says Reinfurt. Eventually, the ad also appeared in the *San Francisco Chronicle*, *Jerusalem Post*, and a Beirut newspaper. "The ad became a self-sustaining economy, as each ad generated the revenue to run the next ad, and so the project gained greater and greater exposure." Reinfurt compares the project to a: "Low-tech, high-concept chain letter for peace."

Wieden+Kennedy

"Graphic design, when used in a creative intelligent manner, will always be a means of improving the quality of our lives," says John Jay, executive creative director and partner at advertising agency Wieden+Kennedy. "It is the visual ability to create emotional connections, and is a recognition and celebration of the complexities and simplicities of the human spirit. Design is not about whether it's modern or not; it's all about how we choose to live our lives."

Jay joined the agency in 1993 as creative director and, in 1998, he moved to Japan to open Wieden+Kennedy Tokyo, where he served as co-executive creative director. In 2004, he moved back to Portland to join Dan Wieden in overseeing the agency globally. "Through design, one can change whole organizations, the way they think, and their standards." And having worked with some of the world's best-known organizations and brands, Jay should certainly know.

Jay was categorical in his ambitions for the Tokyo office of Wieden+Kennedy. He wanted to build what he calls: "A creatively led agency unlike any other, with no separation between above- or below-the-line concepts." Rather than being a regular office, he wanted it to be "a catalyst for creative people from all over the world." Under his direction, the office made innovative use of all media, including design, architecture, and cellphone technology. It also connected many interesting artists to each other through various projects that extended well beyond the realm of traditional advertising.

The W+K Tokyo office works as a meeting place for people with different creative skills contributing to various assignments. For the Nike Presto Instant Go two-minute video, for example, the office offered street artist, David Ellis, a.k.a. Skwerm, what Jay calls "a chance to take his art off the 2D wall and to move it through time and space." Jay assembled a team of post-graffiti artists from Tokyo and Hong Kong, the motion graphic design firm Motion Theory, and DJ Uppercut of Tokyo, to join Ellis, who was appointed artistic director of the project. The resulting video, visceral and visually innovative, was used to promote new Nike technology and the Presto shoe throughout Asia.

Despite the fact that Jay has lived on both coasts of the US and in Tokyo, and spends a large proportion of his time traveling the globe, he has an uncanny acuity for tapping into the specific cultural vibrations of a place or sensibility and articulating them visually, aurally, and emotionally.

"Tokyo is the cradle of manga and anime," says Jay. "Here illustration has been a powerful tool to evoke provocative thought in Japanese society. In Japan, there was never an issue of whether the art of drawing was passè...it's too important to society to suffer from such whims."

"It is paramount that you identify the audience for a project," he says, "because only then can you determine which insights are relevant and how deep you need to go in order to accomplish your communications goal. That target influences your media choices as well as executional tone. How well you know this audience and target helps the creative idea to be conceptually and culturally relevant."

Above: Packaging for DJ Uppercut's "Pieces"
In 2003, John Jay launched W+K Tokyo Lab, an independent music label featuring the most influential young musical talents of Tokyo, who he paired with international visual artists for the creation of packaging and videos. Each release includes a DVD and CD in a collector's package and the videos appear regularly on music television channels in Japan.

Next page: *Attack of the Ninja* video from "Pieces"
The video was directed by Eric Cruz. It uses the visual language of Asian shadow puppets recontextualized through contemporary animation.

Packaging for Hifana albums "Fresh Push Breakin" (top) and "Channel H" (bottom)

"Fresh Push Breakin'" helped to launch Wieden + Kennedy's music label W+K Tokyo Lab. The album's key track, "Fat Bros" inspired the music video directed by W+K's Eric Cruz, which helped to shape the surprising visual language that W+K Tokyo Lab introduced to Tokyo. With the second album, "Channel H," Hifana and W+KTokyoLab ventured into even more surprising territory— both musically and visually. W+K produced 13 original videos, interstitial graphics and animation, as well as the packaging of the music.

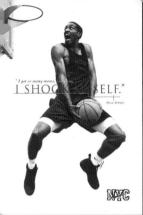

NYC

"I'm like Baskin Robbins, I got 31
SCOOPS."

Earl "The Goat" Manigault

Nike Flow campaign
The Nike Flow basketball campaign was aimed at an Asian demographic. Wieden+Kennedy Tokyo collaborated with LA's Motion Theory and Korean-born street artist Rostarr to produce a spot that used bold patterns to illustrate the flow of teamwork in a basketball game.

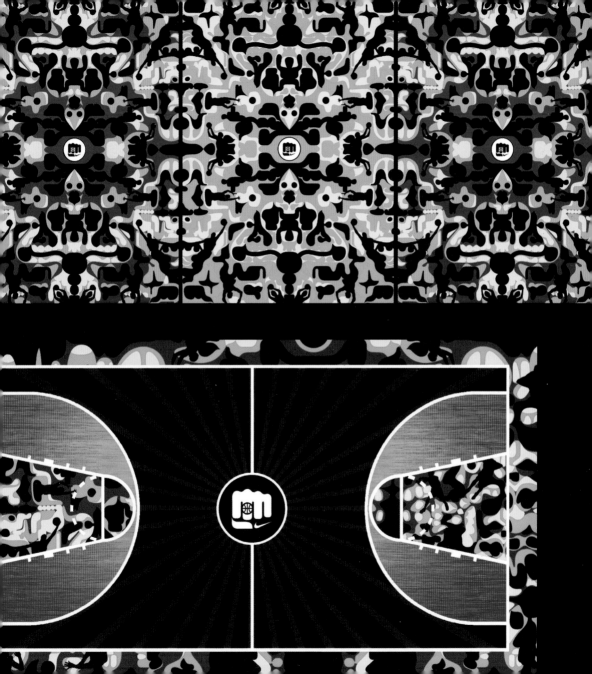

LUST

Thomas Castro and Jeroen Barendse founded LUST in 1996, based on a shared interest in concepts such as coincidence, non-hierarchical and generative systems, and the potential of emerging technologies. In 1999, they were joined by Dimitri Nieuwenhuizen, who brings interactive design experience to the Dutch studio.

Important design strategies for LUST include process-based design, mapping, and the role of coincidence and chance elements. "Although we are technically Generation X, we feel more part of Generation Random," they say.

LUST reinvestigates the stipulations of given formats for the delivery of information, all across the high- to low-tech spectrum. From mapping and cartographic exercises for architectural clients and Dutch ministries, to unique interactive information systems for major museums; from postage stamps and book and catalog design, to complex interactive spatial interventions. All projects represent LUST's interest in the frontier where nonlinear informational structures and process-led methodologies meet traditional design craftsmanship and typography.

Through Digital Depot, for example, LUST re-envisioned the museum information display. A permanent exhibition space at Rotterdam's Museum Boijmans van Beuningen showcases a revolving selection of 60 to 80 works of art that are presented on a large wall. In front of these works of art hang six panels of glass, or transparent interfaces, which display information about the art when activated by touch. In the same room is DataCloud, a spatial visualization of the real-time database of 117,000 works of art in the entire Boijmans collection. The interactive digital environment is navigable with a joystick.

For the city of Hoek Van Holland, the group reexamined the map format. The map was intended to show the many facets of Hoek van Holland and was published on the occasion of the Rotterdam 2001: Cultural Capital festival. It had to contain a great deal of information—historical, economic, industrial, residential, maritime, and recreational—and ended up, therefore, being 6 ½ feet (2 meters) long. LUST devised a folding system that eliminated the trouble of having to continually fold and refold the map to see the necessary information. It can be used as four maps of increasing detail: going from the world, to Europe, to the North Sea, and finally to Hoek van Holland. Each folded variant shows information pertaining to that specific area, as well as showing its relationship to the bigger area around it.

LUST works with a typically Dutch array of clients, including architects and city planners, publishers, music groups, galleries, fine art institutions, various small cultural entities, as well as larger institutions, Dutch ministries and municipalities, and national museums. LUST enjoys the specificity of the audiences that they design for. "We could make the publicity for an art and technology festival broadly communicative (by just putting the name of the thing as big as possible on a poster)," says Barendse. A better strategy, in his opinion, is to celebrate the specialist nature of this audience. "This allows us to go further than we would be able to with a normal campaign."

LUST Web site

Visitors to LUST's Web site are greeted by a pattern of interwoven images of what is currently on the computer desktops of the studio members, combined, sliced, and mediated through an intense pixelation process. A software program called EvoCam watches, records, and distorts the desktops every five minutes as LUST members continue with their daily work. These screenshots are then processed using a custom software program that LUST developed to slice, block, and create the mixed desktop images.

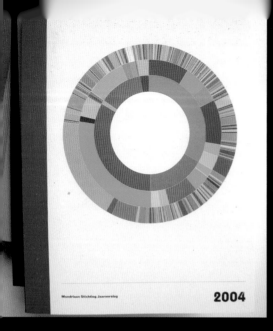

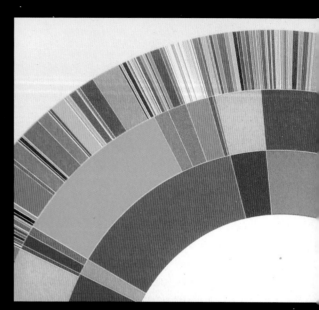

Mondriaan Stichting Jaarverslag

2004

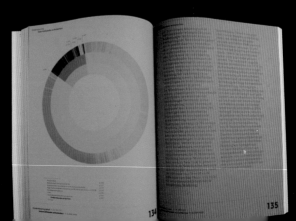

134 135

Mondriaan Foundation annual report

The Mondriaan Foundation was created to stimulate visual arts, design, and the cultural heritage of the Netherlands. It offers financial support to enable institutions, companies, and authorities—both national and international—to reach their audiences. The Foundation's annual report gives information about the thousand-plus projects they helped to finance, ranging in scale from as little as a hundred to millions of euros. LUST devised a typographical system that separates different levels of information. Chapter dividers feature maps showing the locations of supported projects, and three-ring pie charts that show exactly what has been spent on each project. The cover is printed in eight different colors and every page is printed on a different colored paper, selected randomly from a spectrum of 20, ensuring that each copy of the report is unique.

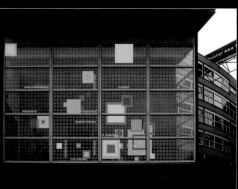

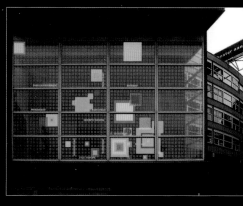

Filmhuis map and information screen

LUST was commissioned by The Hague art cinema (Filmhuis) to transform their public façade into a map and information screen. With neither the budget for an LCD or LED installation, nor the desire to use the window as an opaque screen (this would block the view for those within), they came up with a solution that mixes low technology and high concept. They applied semiopaque vinyl film squares in a grid pattern representing venues in The Hague that were part of the "TodaysArt" festival, and used a standard high-lumen projector to project onto the individual vinyl squares, creating an overall pattern across the façade.

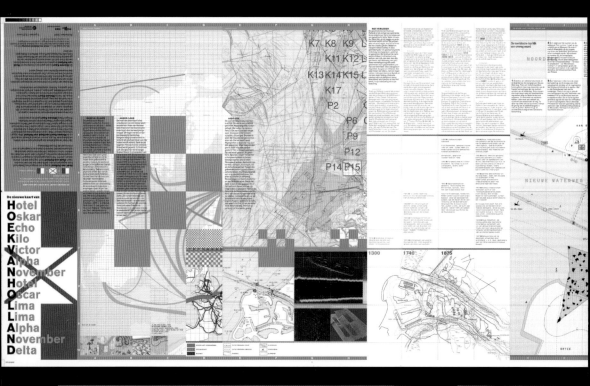

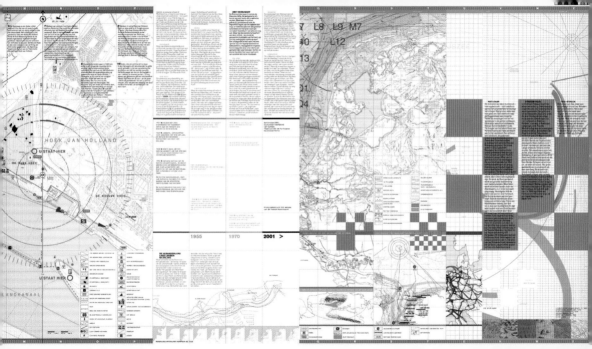

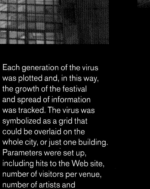

"TodaysArt" festival identity
LUST puts new technologies at the very center of its work and sees how they can influence and guide the form and look of whatever it is they are creating. In the case of an identity for an art, music, and technology festival, such a strategy seemed particularly appropriate. Using the idea of a virus as a means of replicating and spreading information as their inspiration and organizing principle, LUST created a generative program that was used to affect and guide all aspects of the festival identity: from the graphic language to the means of spreading information. The virus resided on the festival Web site and could be viewed at all times. Installations throughout the city also served as barometers for the virus.

Each generation of the virus was plotted and, in this way, the growth of the festival and spread of information was tracked. The virus was symbolized as a grid that could be overlaid on the whole city, or just one building. Parameters were set up, including hits to the Web site, number of visitors per venue, number of artists and performances playing, and the locations of interventions, and the data affected by the grid.

Frédéric Teschner

"I think that the best things I have created are those that gave me the most pleasure in the process," says Frédéric Teschner. "I have the desire to progress very quickly, because anyway, no one gets out of here alive."

Born in Thiais, France, Frédéric Teschner graduated from the École Nationale Supérieure des Arts Décoratifs (ENSAD) in Paris. He began working with experimental typographer Pierre di Sciullo, then with designer Pierre Bernard, both of whom used to work in the politically motivated French design group, Grapus. Those collaborations encouraged Teschner to challenge his own methods of exploring the possibilities of graphic design, to master several means of expression—drawing, photography, and typography—and various types of visual communication, such as posters, books, and exhibition signage.

"What is more specific to my practice is that I regularly work in collaboration with someone else. The most important thing for me is not to create a project for a specific audience; it is to find the best and most original way to respond to a command. The best way to transmit a message, an état d'esprit (mindset). If you carefully listen to the client, you can often discover the components of an answer in the description of the problem. A pertinent, precise, contemporary, and remarkable response is always well received by the audience."

Teschner has been working solo since 2000 in Montreuil, a suburb outside of Paris known for its rich cultural community. "I like this town," he says. "It's very mixed socially, and I had the opportunity to rent a larger space for less money than I would have paid in Paris." Since he has been working in Montreuil, he finds that his work has become more deeply connected with art, design, and architecture. Among his projects that concern design are a poster for the Ronan and Erwan Bouroullec exhibition at the Design Museum in London, a monograph for the designer Martin Szekely, and an installation in the Villa de Noailles with the designer Jean-François Dingjian.

In 2003, he designed the signage and the exhibition catalog for "Signes des Écoles d'Art" at the Centre Pompidou. This was the starting point of a regular collaboration with the Pompidou. In 2004, he conceived the signage, exhibition catalog, and journals for a brand new exhibition space within the Centre that is dedicated to contemporary art.

"I like to work with people of different creative sectors who have respect for and trust in the graphic designer's work," explains Teschner. "This way, the designer can find his own best way to communicate without preconceived ideas. Nonetheless, my first wish is to serve the client's vision, not mine."

les
maîtres
d'art

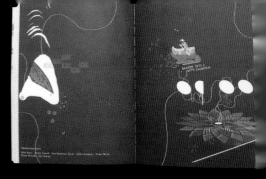

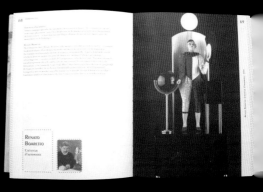

**Les Maîtres d'Art cover
and spreads**
This book, published by
the Ministry of Culture, is a
celebration of the traditional
craft industries of France.

315
espace trois-cent-quinze

Magnus von Plessen

Kristin Baker

9 juin / 23 août 2004

Centre Pompidou, Espace 315 signage, catalogs, and journals
"For the catalogs, I created a simple and spare graphic system," says Teschner. "The cover keeps back the reproduced work and enhances the artist's name to create a sort of visual enigma. This specificity lends mystery to the cover, attracting the audience's attention. At the same time, this visual identity is strong enough to lay the foundation for a new series of books. The small format is in keeping with the book's purpose as a working tool."

LE JOURNAL DU 315

NUMÉRO 2 AUTOMNE/HIVER FALL/WINTER 2004

Centre Pompidou

315
espace trois-cent-quinze

www.centrepompidou.fr

ÉDITO

"Les Dentiers Lumineux"
exhibition signage (left)
and invitation (right)
Teschner designed signage
for this international designers
exhibition that took place in
Cologne, Germany.

Graphisme en France
publication and
Web site
The French Ministry of
Culture's annual publication
about the French graphic
design industry.

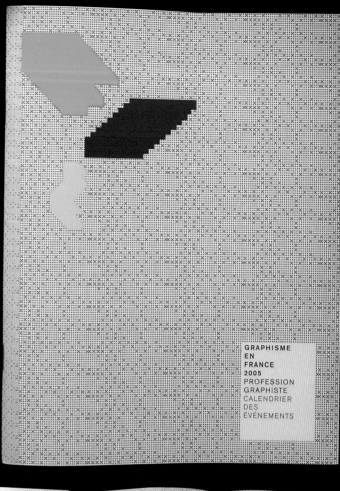

GRAPHISME
EN
FRANCE
2005
PROFESSION
GRAPHISTE
CALENDRIER
DES
ÉVÉNEMENTS

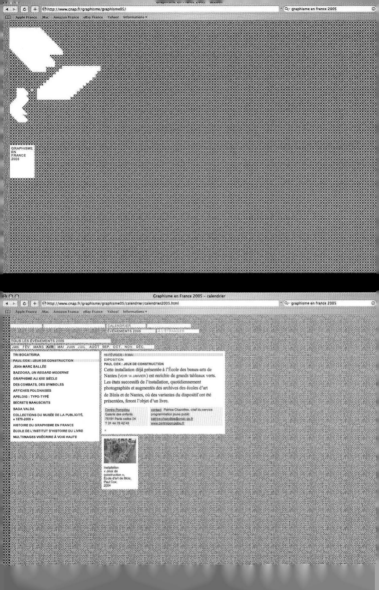

Open

"I feel like students think that all of their beautiful rationalizations need to be consciously evident in their work when the viewer looks at it—but they don't." says Scott Stowell, proprietor of the New York-based design studio, Open. "I do think you should have a reason for everything you make, even if it's that you don't want to have a reason, and I do believe that all your historical research and ideas should go into the making of your work but, in most cases, the viewer is going to look at it and read the content— that's it. If they get anything else out of it, [that] might be something entirely different than what you put into it. You need to be ready for that, or better yet, actually enjoy it."

Stowell established Open in 1998, its mission, simple yet enduring, is to: "Help people figure out what they need to say, and use design to say it in ways that surprise, engage, and inform." Open has enjoyed steady success and has worked for clients in culture, entertainment, and politics. The firm is small with just Stowell, two designers, and a studio manager on payroll, but, with access to a large network of talent, it is able to expand as the scale of a project necessitates. Projects include redesigns of the TV networks Bravo, Nick At Nite, and Trio; a comprehensive signage program for the Yale University Art Gallery; and an ongoing series of short films for Jazz at Lincoln Center's Hall of Fame.

"I constantly want to put myself in the shoes of the actual person who is going to use the thing I'm designing," says Stowell, whose studio tagline is "Design for People." "I try to create an agenda that serves that person first, and then the client," he goes on. "You have to serve the client, of course, but the reason they're asking you to make something in the first place is because of the people that will use or experience it. Nine times out of ten, clients don't remember that, or think about it, or make choices based upon it." Stowell thinks of the designer as an advocate for the person who is on the receiving end of design, but who can't really speak for him or herself. "They don't know anything about typefaces or design history or theory, but they're not stupid," he says. "They look at design at face value to see what information there is to get out of it, what it looks like and how it makes them feel."

Being mindful of the person who will use his work, does not mean that Stowell agrees with market research. In fact he sees it as a, "Total waste." In his view, the limitations of focus groups come from: "The kinds of questions that are asked. Market researchers feel the need to create a group where there isn't one.

"Sometimes, I think you also have to confront people with things they don't understand," says Stowell. "People don't know what they're going to like or respond to until they see it. But it tends to be the thing that feels new and pure and driven—the thing with integrity."

Stowell equates experiencing a piece of well-considered graphic design with receiving a present: "You feel really special and that the giver cared about you. I love looking at design where you get the sense that the designers really went for it. Even if it's really bad. Some cyber-punk Kentucky Fried Chicken packaging? If they really cared, then why not?"

EarthAction campaign
Starting with the Children's
Rights Campaign, Open
developed a new visual
identity and editorial point
of view for EarthAction and
used them to make posters,
postcards, action kits, and

clarinetist and saxophonist

Sidney Bechet

trane

1926-1967

Saxophonist John Coltrane

This page and following page: *Jazz at Lincoln Center Hall of Fame* films
Open created 26 biographical films about the greats of jazz—such as Ella Fitzgerald, King Oliver, and Thelonius Monk—who had been inducted into the Jazz Hall of Fame. The animations are shown on a 21 by 4 feet (6.4 by 1.2 meter) grid of videos along one wall of a public lobby area in the Jazz at Lincoln Center building in New York. The one-and-a-half to three-minute films were supposed to be both an abstract interpretation of the music and an informative historical resume of the musician's career. "Jazz has either really hard core fans or people that dismiss it very easily. So we had those two groups of people to serve," says Stowell. Open chose to focus on the people that needed converting.

Each film includes: a quote from the musician, the name of the song, who recorded it, the date, a four-sentence biography, historical photos, film footage, and album covers. On top of this, Open created for each artist a photographic concept and an illustrative concept that reflected their character or style of playing. For Billy Holliday, for example, they used photographic images of gardenias because she wore them in her hair. The illustrative concept uses trees and leaves to make lyrical patterns but also to reference Holiday's rendition of "Strange Fruit," the famous poem about lynching. The final element in the film is the way in which the various parts mix together in time with or in syncopation with the music. "We talked about how, if music has these different variables such as tempo, technique, and pitch, and so on, then the design has corresponding variables," says Stowell. "Do they fade, or cut or slide or how do they move?"

Even though they were creating enormous frames which, at 5,600 by 1,200 pixels, are 14 times the size of a normal frame, Open were able to produce everything in its office using G5s. The films make liberal use of flat colors and hard shapes to cut down on memory. Another esthetic choice that became a technical advantage was the fact that Stowell wanted to achieve the look of classic print and banned "trippy, Photoshoppy effects," again cutting down on rendering time. The rule he gave to the animators was: "If you couldn't have made it in film, don't do it."

"The **piano** ain't got **no** wrong **notes!**"

has been uplifting people with his music

Trio identity

Trio is a TV network for true fans of popular culture. Open created a changing tagline to go with the network's new logo (by design studio No.17) and with the help of collaborators (like filmmaker Chris Wilcha and music supervisors Agoraphone) Open developed a new identity for Trio, including the copy, design, animation, sound design, and music. Open produced IDs, menus that appear to sort shows like a search engine, a new look for their Web site, and a style guide.

triotv.com

A **TRIO** Live Presentation

A **TRIO** Original Production

We think that
you should know:

This next show contains language that's not for kids.

TRIC standards,
practices,
tv.

triotv.com

search:
box office

Sat 5pm (et)

Easy Riders/
Raging Bulls
Superman: The Movie
Christopher Reeve

Sat 8pm (et)

Face Time wit
Kurt Anderse
Peter Bart

TRIC popcorn,
soda,
tv.

"Should a designer design for a factory in which he could never imagine working as an operative? Is design social-realist art? Is it handy to be in a state of moral grace when designing a knife and fork? Should a designer be a conformist or an agent of change?" These are some of the questions with which designer and writer Norman Potter winnowed the readers from the non-readers in the first chapter of his *What is a Designer?: Things, Places, Messages* (2002, HyphenPress). Those that thought such questions: "Diversionary and a waste of time," were advised to put the book down. Those who were intrigued were invited to: "Read on, but not for easy answers." John Morgan, who encountered the book several decades after it was written, read on. In fact, the questions posed in the book continue to shape his practice.

After graduating from the Typography and Graphic Communication course at the University of Reading, Morgan moved to London and worked for four years with Derek Birdsall at Omnific Studios, London, primarily on books for clients such as the Arts Council of England, Channel 4 Television, and Yale University Press. Morgan and Birdsall also collaborated on redesigning the prayer book for the Church of England. In 2000, Morgan established his own practice, centered, at first, on editorial design for Booth-Clibborn Editions, Mike Figgis's studio Red Mullet, Thames & Hudson, and Ambit Magazine, and then broadening to include public art commissions for clients such as the BBC. In addition to his design work, Morgan writes for design journals including *Typography Papers* and *Dot Dot Dot*. His manifesto, the

"Vow of Chastity," which he produced as a visiting tutor to Central Saint Martins, was reprinted in *Looking Closer 4*. In 2004, Morgan was joined by Michael Evidon, an ex-student from Saint Martins.

In his book, Potter notes that: "Designer are ordinary human beings" and, when Morgan is asked about graphic design's purpose, he points out that: "Most 'graphic design' is done by nonprofessionals, by people who wouldn't call themselves a 'graphic designer.' A secretary designing a PowerPoint presentation, a shopkeeper handwriting a window sign. For them, as for me, it's about getting a message across

Morgan believes that graphic design is, at its best, a social activity. This explains his "Predilection for books and what they stan for." There's no glib definition for the role of what he calls this "invented profession," however. "How can graphic design be a responsible trade when we don't create the content, and we convey somebody else's message? The key is to find an area of desig that offers some experience of authenticity

He may have found such an area in his work for the BBC. The BBC's press release refer to the projects as "public art," yet Morgan continues to think of them as desig rather than art. "As a designer, I am primaril concerned with the problems of the client or the community rather than just with developing my own body of work," he says "I come from the unfashionable school of thought where what I do is 'work,' and whe there 'is art in everything I do.' It always seems a little absurd when somebody calls themselves an artist. Art is always and everywhere, as Eric Gill might say."

The Invisible University and its historical values:

I. U. means learning as an·ecosystem
(what on earth might this mean?).

I. U. means being carbon positive.

I. U. all data is everywhere, all the time.

I. U. means architecture is no substitute for
face-to-face contact.

I. U. means a new relationship between
man and nature.

I. U. needs no new buildings.

I. U. means tune up kits
(small robots, cyber-pets and
neuro-gardening – see catalogue
available from caretaker).

I. U. means knowing what time it is, is more
important than knowing where you are.

I. U. uses less fuel per hour
than any other university.

I. U.

Invisible University poster
The prospectus for the
Invisible University proposes
a new model for future
architectural education. It
is written by ex-Archigram
member David Greene
who, along with Samantha
Hardingham, commissioned
Morgan to create this
silkscreened poster.

BBC – Voices of White City hoarding project

This large-scale community-focused artwork is made up of 10,000 stickers, each one bearing an individual poem stuck on to a 328-foot (100-meter) hoarding that runs along a street at the BBC Media Village at White City. BBC staff and local residents participated in workshops led by established writers and the resulting poems are about the participants' lives—their connections, their conflicts, their pasts, and their futures. En masse, the stickers spell out the phrase "Voices of White City," and passers-by are invited to peel off any poem and reattach it somewhere else. Passers-by include those who use the supermarket located on the street, children on the way home from school, and BBC staff.

Morgan saw the stickers travel to the train station, to a school, and to the BBC wine bar. "One kid covered the wall of his bedroom, others stuck them on bags, clothes, cars, CCTV posts, sidewalks, windows, and bus stops." Morgan observed that people seemed to choose their favorite phrase—the most popular choice was "we are gifted souls"—or take one for a friend. The way in which the stickers were dispersed gave the project life beyond the hoarding; the texts quite literally made their way into the community. As Robert Seatter, BBC Project Manager, says: "The ultimate aspiration was always that this work would find its way into the landscape so it could be reflected back to the community from where it came.

"But the additional innovation is John Morgan's wonderful hoarding design, which invites people to peel off any poem they take a liking to. Who knows how far some of these poems will travel?" Initially, Morgan wanted to affix a large digital print to the hoarding but the estimated cost of cleaning the surface and laminating the print came in at around 20 times the modest budget. The answer was to produce something which could be repeated and work in a modular grid system. "The final result was actually cheaper than the quote I got for paint the hoarding white!" recalls Morgan. "As always, the given constraint produced the solution and worked in my favor."

BBC "Voices of White City" sidewalk project

A collaboration between BBC staff and community participants intended to create better understanding between the BBC and its local community and to give that understanding a tangible voice. Several pieces of public art have emerged from the project so far, including this collaboration between Andrew Motion, the British Poet Laureate, and John Morgan.

The five couplets of a poem are laid in granite sett panels that run 321 feet (98 meters) along the length of the public street, between BBC office buildings, in a landscape designed by Christopher Bradley-Hole. The scale is such that, in Morgan's words, "It's as if the landscape has begun to speak for itself." Here was an opportunity, in a prosaically inclined world, for poetry to be an intrinsic part of the landscape and building pattern. Letterforms are created using a variation in stone color (intensified by rainfall). Silver granite setts in place are replaced with darker granite.

Building elements are like pixels, the resulting image the bitmap—an esthetic inextricably linked to computer technology, though long-served in mosaics and embroidery. This coarse grid was, in turn, a constraint passed onto the poet who had a maximum of 14 characters per line to work with. All five couplets of the walkway poem, when translated into a binary system, fit into one panel. Zeros and ones become silver and gray granite stones, creating a mathematical basis for a geometric design.

"Behind The Glass" project

When BBC staff and their children participated in a one-day writing workshop conducted by children's author Vivian French, Morgan was asked to think of a way the texts the children generated could be visualized at the end of the session. The solution had to be cheap, quick to produce, fun and child-friendly. Morgan observed that the BBC building is covered in glass and that the room the workshop took place in faced the street.

Knowing from his own experience how much people like to draw faces and letters on windows, and wanting to continue the theme of public lettering inspired by the everyday (begun in the Voices of White City Project), he decided to cover the windows in a window cleaning product and invite parents and children to apply their texts using stencils and brushes. It also occurred to Morgan that, from the street, it looked as if the children were trapped inside a giant TV and, to continue this analogy, he created a test card at one end of the window, made with the different tools and stencils, to demonstrate to the children what kind of marks they could make.

Experiments in Architecture
Experiments in Architecture
Experiments in Architecture
Experiments in Architecture
Experiments in Architecture
Experiments in Architecture
Experiments in Architecture
Experiments in Architecture
Experiments in Architecture
Experiments in Architecture
Experiments in Architecture
Experiments in Architecture
Experiments in Architecture
Experiments in Architecture
Experiments in Architecture
Experiments in Architecture
Experiments in Architecture
Experiments in Architecture
Edited by Samantha Hardingham
Published by August, London

***Experiments in Architecture* title page, spread, and cover**
This book, edited by Samantha Hardingham is, says Morgan, "very much a 'What is Architecture For?' book and contains short stories, letters, and notes written by architects, artists, educationalists, design tutors, clients, makers, and developers.

Excerpts from the script for
THE WORLD'S LAST HARDWARE EVENT – 1970
A four-screen multimedia presentation.

Imagine a landscape and imagine these people sitting there – they are in a bottery. The bottery is part of the idea of space park earth.

DEFINITION:

A BOTTERY IS A FULLY SERVICED NATURAL LANDSCAPE.

THE BOT:

MACHINE- TRANSIENT IN THE LANDSCAPE.

References

Issues

What is graphic design for?
What Is Design For? A discussion, Michael
Bierut; *Design Observer*
www.designobserver.com (12:00PM August
17, 2004)

Being here: local tendencies in graphic design
"Being Here: Craft and Locality in Graphic
Design" GraficEurope conference, Berlin
(October, 2004)
Zembla, Simon Finch,
www.zemblamagazine.com
Emigre, www.emigre.com
BEople, www.beople.be
Re-Magazine, www.re-magazine.com

Cross-disciplinary design and collaboration
Art Center College of Design, Pasadena, CA,
US, www.artcenter.edu
Design Studies, Central Saint Martins
College of Art and Design, London, UK,
www. csm.arts.ac.uk

Designer as author, publisher, producer, curator, entrepreneur
"American Graphic Design Expression,"
Katherine McCoy, *Design Quarterly* 149
(MIT Press, 1990)
"The Designer as Author," Michael Rock, *Eye*
No. 20 (Spring 1996)
Massive Change, www.massivechange.com
Designer as Author MFA Program, School of
Visual Arts, New York, NY, US,
design.schoolofvisualarts.edu

Dot Dot Dot, Stuart Bailey and Peter Bilak,
Amsterdam, the Netherlands,
www.dot-dot-dot.nl
The Riviera Gallery, Brooklyn, NY, US,
www.seeyouattheriviera.com
Winterhouse Editions, Falls Village, CT, US,
www.winterhouse.com
Design Observer, Michael Bierut, William
Drentell, Jessica Helfand, and Rick Poynor,
www.designobserver.com
Browns Books, London, UK,
www.brownsdesign.com
F7 lecture series, Paris, France,
www.fsept.net
Green Lady, www.greenlady.com
HunterGatherer, www.huntergatherer.net
Stereohype, www.stereohype.com

Design for protest
Robbie Conal's Art Attack,
www.robbieconal.com
"First Things First" manifesto, (1964)
Ken Garland, www.kengarland.co.uk
AIGA National Design Conference 2005,
designconference.aiga.org
TrueMajority, www.truemajority.org
Natalie Jeremijenko's Feral Robots,
xdesign.ucsd.edu/feralrobots
Bikes Against Bush,
www.bikesagainstbush.com
Flrt, www.flat.com/projects/flrt.html
Okay News, www.famousmime.com

Sustainability

Treehugger, www.treehugger.com
SuperNaturale, www.supernaturale.com
The Power of Design: AIGA National Design
Conference 2003, powerofdesign.aiga.org

Craft and complexity

"The Macrame of Resistance,"
Lorraine Wild, *Emigre 47* (1998)
Design Research: Methods and Perspectives,
ed. Brenda Laurel (MIT Press, 2003)
Why Not Associates? 2, Alice Twemlow,
Rocco Rondondo, Andy Altmann, David Ellis
(Thames and Hudson, 2004)
"Decorationism," Jason A. Tselentis,
Speak Up,
www.underconsideration.com/speakup
(November 20, 2004)
Abstracting Craft: The Practiced Digital Hand,
Malcolm McCullough (MIT Press, 1998)
"Toward Definition of the Decorational,"
Denise Gonzales Crisp (MIT Press, year?)
"Beyond Bauhaus," Louise Schouwenberg,
Frame 41 (2004)

Graphic design is for people

"Death of the Author," Roland Barthes,
Image-Music-Text (Hill and Wang, 1978)
The Bubble Project,
www.thebubbleproject.com

Portfolios

barbara says, www.barbarasays.com
Base, www.basedesign.com
COMA, www.comalive.com
deValence, www.devalence.net
Vince Frost, www.emeryfrost.com
Radovan Jenko, *Radovan Jenko Posters,*
(La Look editions, 2005)
Kerr|Noble, www.kerrnoble.com
LUST, www.lust.nl
John Morgan, www.morganstudio.co.uk
Open, www.notclosed.com
ORG, www.o-r-g.com
Frédéric Teschner, fredericteschner.com
Clarissa Tossin, www.a-linha.org
Wieden+Kennedy, www.wiedenkennedy.com
www.wktokyolab.com
Martin Woodtli, www.woodt.li

*Fresh Dialogue 3, New Voices in Graphic
Design,* ed. Veronique Vienne (Princeton
Architectural Press, 2004)
*Fresh Dialogue 5, New Voices in Graphic
Design,* ed. Veronique Vienne, (Princeton
Architectural Press, 2005)
Chaumont 2005, Pyramid, 2005
Rant Nos. 64 and 65, (*Emigre* and Princeton
Architectural Press, 2004)

Glossary

authorship

A word that began to be used in the same sentence as graphic design in the 1980s, as designers explored the potential of literary theory for their own work and its interpretation. In 1990 Katherine McCoy, director at the Cranbrook Academy of Art, invoked the term "author" very specifically, for its literary resonance: "By authoring additional content and a self-conscious critique of the message, they [her students] are adopting roles associated with both art and literature." Tutors and students did not set out to solve communication problems, so much as present the viewer with a communication problem to solve. The role of the audience in the design process was prioritized. More recently, the definition has expanded to embrace the concepts of entrepreneurship and production–designers who are taking control of the conditions of making, in order to create new products and ideas, to initiate new economies for creative practice.

avant-garde

During the first few decades of the 20th-century various groups of artists throughout Europe and America included decorative arts, design, and graphic design as integral parts of their defining philosophies. The pamphlets, posters, and manifestos that they published have since become defining artifacts in the graphic design canon. The proto-graphic designers associated with these avant-garde movements reacted with various levels of intensity to the condition of the modern mechanical age and to war. The word avant-garde comes from the French and means front guard or vanguard. Those at the avant-garde took risks by creating works or expounding ideas that were innovative, powerful, and that ran counter to dominant ideas of the day. At this time there was an unprecedented level of exchange of new ideas and ways of seeing taking place among artists and designers of different nationalities. Their ideas crossed national, cultural, and linguistic barriers via avant-garde periodicals and advances in travel and communications technology.

blog

This term is a shortened form of Web log. In the past few years increasing numbers of people have initiated their own blogs, or Web sites, through which they generate text, photographs, video or audio files, and/or links, typically on a daily basis. Individual articles on a blog are called "posts," and in most cases the aim is to incite others to respond with "comments" that en masse become a "thread."

craft

Simply put, this term describes skill in making things, and yet graphic design's relationship with it has been anything but simple. Partly because of unglamorous connotations–macramé, crochet, felting, and so on–and partly because of a steady impetus throughout the 20th-century to align graphic design with machines, efficiency, mass production, and problem solving, craft was not a part of design discourse for many years. Recent reexaminations of the value of ornament, complexity, and tacit knowledge in graphic design, however, in combination with a broader popularization of DIY culture and "craftyness," have refocused attention upon making in ways that are proving invigorating for many designers.

dada

Dada began as a literary movement when, after the outbreak of WW1, the poet Hugo Ball started the Cabaret Voltaire in Zurich for young poets. Their formal anti-rationalism was supposed to mirror the anti-rationalism of war and the disorientating experience of living in a modern technological society. While the futurists glorified militarism, dadaists saw war as the ultimate breakdown of Western civilization. This disillusionment led the dadaists to embrace concepts of nonsense and chance in their work that was deliberately political, critical, and absurd. The tools for their attack on cultural values included games of chance, collage, abstraction, audience confrontation, eclectic typography, sound, and visual poetry.

deconstruction

This term was coined by French philosopher Jacques Derrida in 1967, and is used in contemporary humanities and social sciences as a label for exploration of the linguistic and institutional systems that frame the production of texts.

futurism

This early 20th-century movement was led by the poet Filippo Tommaso Marinetti, who wanted to liberate words and meaning from the tight bonds of tradition, and who celebrated speed, machines, and even war. In his 1909 manifesto on futurism, Marinetti declared: "We affirm that a new beauty has enriched the world's magnificence: the beauty of speeds…Except in struggle, there is no more beauty. No work without an aggressive character can be a masterpiece…We will destroy museums, libraries, and fight against moralism, feminism, and all utilitarian cowardice."

globalization

Thanks to the removal of trade barriers, in conjunction with the increasing availability of cutting- edge hardware and software technology, the market for the exchange of goods and services has expanded to a global scale. For many, this "flattening" of the world presents rich opportunities for progress. For others, it represents a breakdown of national autonomy and cultural distinctiveness. Designers are implicated in this tale of technology and geoeconomics at many levels: as the primary creators of brands that can speak across cultures, and as the owners of firms that they'd like to see expand. They can also play a key role in, if not stemming, then at least critiquing the global flow through their sensitivity to the nuances and particular flavors of local culture.

international typography

The predominant convention in graphic design of the late 1960s and 1970s was the Swiss style, or International Typography, derived from European modernism. No decoration, white space, a limited range of typefaces, and strict use of the grid were all characteristics of such design. This approach, claimed by its adherents to be "value free" since it had no historical references, was challenged in the 1980s with the influx of new thinking generated by postmodernism.

mise-en-scène
This term derives from the theater where, in French, mise-en-scène means literally "putting into the scene" or "setting in scene." More popularly understood in relation to the cinema, mise-en-scène refers to everything that appears before the camera and its arrangement—sets, props, actors, costumes, and lighting—and how these elements reflect a mood or a character's state of mind. It is often used in contradistinction to a montage approach to filmmaking in which frames are edited together. Not usually used in conjunction with graphic design, the term provides a way of looking at the work of designers who physically construct scenes and compositions out of materials in a studio and either film or photograph them. The impetus for such a method comes from the designers' dissatisfaction with the slick surfaces and lack of "authenticity" they perceive in many software programs.

modernism
Modernism's roots lie in early 20th-century Germany. The Bauhaus opened in Weimar in 1919 with Walter Gropius as its first director. The various disciplines that were taught were all ultimately in the service of architecture, but the experimental character of the school led to the development of new innovations for graphic design too. Students and teachers such as Laszlo Moholy-Nagy and Herbert Bayer expanded the possibilities for image-making and typography. Posters and books produced to promote various aspects of the school display the principles of modernist design such as clarity, objectivity, asymmetry, and the emphatic use of lower-case, sans serif type and photography. The reasons why modernism has dominated the way graphic design is practiced and thought about

for so long, are numerous and complicated. One of the reasons is the way in which its proponents were dispersed due to the rise of Fascism in Europe in the 1930s and 1940s. Many were forced to emigrate to the US. Here designers such as Moholy-Nagy, Ladislav Sutnar, Josef Albers, and Hans Richter found acceptance in the corporate sphere and many of them took prominent positions at existing schools or set up their own, leading to a cultural osmosis of their ideas and methods.

news agate
A standard unit of measurement found primarily in newspaper publishing. Agate is approximately equal to 5 1/2 points, 1/14 of an inch, or 1.814 millimeters. Such small type tends to be used for statistical data in the sports and stock sections of a newspaper. Agate presents peculiar challenges to the type designer. In addition to the narrow measure of the agate column and the fact that the content is dense, succinct, and relies on abbreviations, one also has to factor in the way in which ink spreads and pools in counters when printed on newsprint.

sans serif
In typography, a sans serif typeface is one that does not have the small angled or oblique feet called "serifs" at the end of letter strokes. First introduced by William Caslon IV in 1816, sans serif type, or Egyptian as it was called then, was reserved almost exclusively for headlines.

VJ
VJs are a new breed of visual practitioner—equal parts filmmaker, designer, and performer—who mix and project imagery at clubs, in response to the music that's being played.

Index

Credits

My heartfelt thanks go to the following:

My partner in life and crime David
Womack for all he has contributed
to this book;

My talented editorial assistants and
collaborators Gina Cherry and
Samantha Topol;

All at RotoVision especially Jane Roe
and Jane Waterhouse whose patience
and dedication I truly appreciate;

Quentin Newark, author of the first
book in this series *What is Graphic
Design?*, for his kind counsel;

And all the brilliant designers who
have generously contributed their
work and thoughts to this book
and who continue to inspire me.

Production: America's Answer by Jean
Carlu © ADAGP, Paris and DACS,
London 2006